THE THIRD COAST

THE THIRD COAST

CONTEMPORARY MICHIGAN POETRY

edited by

Conrad Hilberry
Kalamazoo College

Herbert Scott
Western Michigan University

James Tipton
Alma College

with a preface by
David Wagoner
University of Washington

Wayne State University Press
Detroit, 1976

Library of Congress Cataloging in Publication Data

Main entry under title:

   The Third coast.

   1. American poetry—Michigan.   2.   American poetry—20th century.
I.   Hilberry, Conrad.   II.   Scott, Herbert, 1931–   III.   Tipton, James,
1942–
PS571.M5T5   811'.5'408   76-49581
ISBN 0-8143-1567-4
ISBN 0-8143-1568-2 pbk.

Grateful acknowledgment is made to the Michigan Council for the Arts,
whose financial assistance has made possible the publication of this volume.

Permissions

        Acknowledgment is made for permission to reprint the poems listed below.
Michael Delp. "Living with the Fat Man," sections of "Uncle," originally in *Wind* magazine.
Barbara Drake. "Old Folk Tale," © 1972 by *Michigan Hot Apples;* "The Ancestors" and "She
    Dreams Herself Titanic," originally in *Sumac;* "Case History," *10 Michigan Poets,* ed. Eric
    Greinke, © 1972 by Pilot Press Books; "Good Friends and First Impressions," © 1975 by *Red
    Cedar Review;* "The Woman Gets Restless," © 1971 by *Centennial Review;* "Magic Children,"
    © 1975 by Barbara Drake, originally in *Northwest Review.*
Stuart Dybek. "Vivaldi," © 1974 by *Goddard Journal;* "Night of Voyeurs," © 1976 by *Ohio
    Review;* "The Poems of the Condemned Man," originally in *New York Quarterly.*
Hugh Fox. " 'Christ, that was a real one,' he said" and "His reaction to her asking for a divorce,"
    originally published in *The Mid Atlantic Review;* "There was something white sticking out of
    the sand," selection from *Apotheosis of Olde Towne,* San Bruno, Calif.: Fat Frog Press, © 1967
    by Hugh Fox.
Dan Gerber. "Homecoming," originally published in *Poetry Now;* "Journal Entry," © 1975 by
    Seizure; "Death and the Pineapple," © 1975 by Dan Gerber, originally in *New Letters;* "Long
    Light," originally published in *Los;* "Yellow," © 1970 by Dan Gerber, originally in *The New
    Yorker;* "The Russian Poem," originally published in *The Red Cedar Review;* "Two Clouds," in
    Michigan Signatures, ed. Al Drake, © 1969 by Quixote Press.
Donald Hall. "Photographs of China," © 1976 by *American Review;* "Kicking the Leaves," ©
    1976 by Donald Hall, originally in *The New York Times;* "O Cheese," © 1976 by Donald Hall,
    originally in *Grove.*
Jim Harrison. "Letters to Yesenin," *Letters to Yesenin,* Fremont, Mich.: Sumac Press, 1973; © 1973
    by Jim Harrison.
Robert Hayden. "Middle Passage," *An Angle of Ascent,* © 1975 by Liveright.
Conrad Hilberry. "Blind Girl on the Sante Fe," © 1975 by *New Letters;* "For Katherine," © 1971
    by *Field* (also in *Rust,* Ohio University Press, 1974); "Harry Houdini at the Hippodrome," ©
    1973 by *Field* (also in *Rust,* Ohio University Press, 1974); "Hunger," © 1974 by *Field;* "Port-
    holes," © 1975 by Conrad Hilberry, originally in *Antaeus;* "Sea," © 1971 by *Sumac* (also in
    Rust, Ohio University Press, 1974).

CONTENTS

There was a time—and not many decades ago—when the task of editing an anthology of Michigan poets would have been simple: a tough-minded critic might have been hard put to find more than a half-dozen poets worth gathering together under the same title. Theodore Roethke spoke plaintively in his notebooks and his letters about the sense of cultural isolation and literary loneliness during his school and university days in Saginaw and Ann Arbor and occasionally pointed out that, looking back even further, the only regional ancestor he honestly owed a poetic debt to was Julia A. Moore, the self-labelled Sweet Singer of Michigan, the undoubted queen of all nineteenth-century bad verse writers.

But the editors of this anthology had to struggle to keep the book to its present substantial dimensions, omitting both poets and poems they were anxious to keep in. The process of culling has been painful for them and no doubt doubly painful for those omitted, but the reader should be aware that he is seeing the results of a large number of difficult choices and should perhaps be grateful that he didn't have to make those choices himself, privately, while reading an even longer book. In all, 165 poets submitted their work, and the thirty survivors are worthy of your closest attention. They come from many different areas of the state, are both young and old, male and female, black and white; some have published widely, some have never published before; but they share a common characteristic: they are trying to write the best poems they possibly can—a ferociously hard, lonely, demanding, sometimes fearful, sometimes ecstatic job—and are frequently succeeding.

Inside these covers you will find the deceptively simple psychological surprises and oddities of Michael Delp; the touching and original dramatic lyrics of Barbara Drake with their sense of the doubleness of daily life; Stuart Dybek's haunting, unsettling use of nightmarish imagery; the prose poems of Hugh Fox, terse, unpredictable, and memorable; Dan Gerber's direct, open-voiced lyricism; the strong, vividly visual poems of Donald Hall, a poet whose fine work over the years is probably familiar to many readers; the good, tough, and anguished prose poems of Jim Harrison; Robert Hayden's deeply moving "Middle Passage" about the slave trade, further reason for him to continue to be called America's best Black poet; the beautifully controlled rhythms and images of Conrad Hilberry, who is already known to a national audience; David James's highly dramatic use of dread and horror emerging from the commonplace; the carefully understated, direct lyrics of Janet Kauffman; Jane Kenyon's surprisingly effective use of a conversational tone that nevertheless keeps its tension; the very inventive, surreal wildness of Faye Kicknosway; the artful, laconic, understated poems of Philip Legler; Tom KcKeown's tightly constructed, epigrammatic lyrics; Judith Minty's apt and striking uses of fresh metaphors; the clear, appealing directness of Cynthia Nibbelink's voice; Howard Norman's remarkable Indian "naming" poems that tell a great deal about the culture of the Swampy Crees in a very brief space; the fresh, muscular expression of the Black experience in the poems of Dudley Randall; Danny L. Rendleman's wry, affecting, sharply observed lyrics; Lawrence Russ's humane and sympathetic treatment of usually unnoticed private pains; Herbert Scott's simultaneously funny and frightening excursions in a supermarket; the quiet, unadorned, yet very effective poems of Eve Shelnutt; Linda Parker's skillful and flexible handling of the short line; Skaidrite Stelzer's vigorous and unpredictable diction, her poems full of original figurative language; Richard W. Thomas's direct renderings of intense personal experience; the wide range of James Tipton's energetic observations on public and private matters; Eric Torgersen's succinct and witty lyrics; Mark Wangberg's unaffected and unembellished, tightly-fashioned poems; and lastly John Woods's evocative and long-familiar voice, always entirely his own, moving with mature ease between outer and inner worlds, his wit having made the difficult passage, now, into wisdom.

As the editor of POETRY NORTHWEST during the last ten years, I have had to read a very large number of poems and have long been aware that something special has been happening in Michigan. It is easy to get the superficial impression that all American poets live either in New York or in California, but I have had the pleasure of publishing about a dozen of the poems in this anthology—those and other work by eight of the thirty poets here represented—and I am grateful to have been given the chance to praise them all directly, to read some of them for the first time, and to introduce them to you.

For the infrequent reader of poetry who picks up this book and thumbs through warily, ready to defend himself against memories of high school or college tests in literature classes, I have a brief word of advice: these poets know what ineffective teachers of literature never find out and never tell their students— namely, that poetry does not consist of its paraphrasable prose meaning but lies in the lovely complex interplay of its sound, rhythm, connotations, and what is ofen left *un*said. So read these aloud and don't be afraid. Poetry is not innately despicable like fascism or rhubarb. It is at least as ancient and honorable and rich an art as music, for instance, and if that "infrequent reader" were to imagine his life without another note of music, he may have some idea of what he is now missing by ignoring poetry, especially that written by his contemporaries.

This group of Michigan poets appears to share the current nation-wide penchant for open forms, for poems that seek, individually, the shapes of their thoughts and the tones of their voices according to what the poems themselves seem to wish for—supposedly a characteristic of a "romantic" attitude rather than a "classical" in which the poets tend to yield to a tradition. These poets are, then, still unsettled, uncomplacent, still willing to search for the untried possibilities of poetry, to be daring, willing to take the chance of appearing or sounding odd for the sake of discovery. A Michigan poet may be, for practical purposes, indistinguishable from an Illinois poet or an Arizona poet (except for subject matter), but the publication of this anthology serves to underline one layer of regional cultural strength, even though these are not regional poets.

They are spokesmen and spokeswomen both for their neighbors and for distant strangers they may never see. They are the dreamers of the tribe, even if the tribe is scattered and may not know they exist yet. And they have been brought together here to offer you what they have discovered about their worlds— which are also yours and mine.

David Wagoner

Michael Delp, born in Greenville in 1948, now lives on the Au Sable River near Grayling, where he teaches alternative education. He has published in several magazines including *South Dakota Review* and *Greenfield Review* and he is associate editor of *Skywriting* magazine. He is currently working on a book-length poem, "A Dream of the Resurrection."

Photo by Steve Clark

Poem for My Father

Sometimes I say things
you would say.
My hands work like yours
when they curve around tools.

We carry our fathers with us
until we reach the other side
of our lives.
There we let them slump
to the ground
and walk away.

Tonight, thinking about us,
every sharp corner in my body
went round.
I picked up an old Barlow knife
you gave me once at Hartwick Pines
and began carving a walking stick.

The other side is steep.
The trails are hidden by ferns.
I will not see you slump
or watch you wonder
where I am headed.
I'll sneak up behind you,
walk where you walk,
wait for the first chance
to show you something that I know.

Love Poem

Is the woman next door
really in love with you?
She sorts through your garbage,
follows you with her camera.
Letters appear under your pillow.
She sends a piece of her skin over.
It is the delicate skin from her ear,
perfumed.
You put the piece of ear
in a blue velvet pouch
and send it back to her.
You want nothing to do with this.
You go back to living,
trying to remember the smell,
the exact angle of the cut.

Living with the Fat Man

1
At twenty-five he left home,
chased Rommel across North Africa,
then came back to join a carnival.
Now he wears his nightmares like a skin,
sees them every day: two-headed babies,
snakes, alligator women.

2
Once, in a stupor, he called for a ride
from the Grand Rapids bus depot.
He said he wanted to dry out.
Sleep a little.
That summer he sold theatre tickets,
read Billboard magazine.
His eyes were always wet.

3
Summer, 1962. Three months
spent drinking whiskey.
He worked around the house,
washed floors, mowed,
painted things.
My grandmother never knew
he kept drinking.
Late in September,
poking through her garage,
I found a whole barrel of empties,
Jim Beam. When he tipped,
the necks cool in his hands,
the carnival danced in his veins.

4
One year his best friend
was the fat man.
In the old pictures
it's easy to see my uncle,

bone thin,
wearing an alpaca sweater.
He always has the look
of a stunned man,
a man who suddenly wakes up,
realizing his life is packed
into one small suitcase.

5
He worked night shows at first.
Sold tickets to see the hermaphrodite.
Felt the crowds go stale,
the easy women passing like birds
in front of his eyes.
Spent long nights driving between towns,
stopping for young boys,
all of them waiting for a look
at the white thighs of Sasha, Indian princess,
who held a long smile.

6
Whitey drove the truck.
Lumbering through the backroads of
Virginia, stopping in small towns
for gas, a cold pop, a quick hustle
with Nelda, the three-legged wonder.
25¢.
He'd lead the old men up close,
charge an extra quarter
to touch her.

7
Stearns Kentucky.
For three weeks mountain people
came for miles, walked
into a hot green tent.
My uncle sat in front
hawking tickets. 50¢.

Pay a dollar and stay all day.
Sixteen babies floated in jars.
No one knew their names.
No one asked.

8
At the Ionia Free Fair
we always rode the tilt-a-whirl,
ate cotton candy,
then walked through the backs
of the sideshows.
I wanted to crawl
under the burlesque tent.
I remember the music, the drums,
imagined flashes of skin,
fringe moving in a slow, sweet motion,
hips pushing against hard smoky air.

9
Walking through the midway,
the carnies, no teeth,
pregnant women always near them.
I wanted him to play the games.
He winked. Stepped up.
Worked the dice.
His hands knew the corners.
He rolled and won. Rolled and won,
all afternoon.

10
He comes home every year
for the fourth.
His hands tremble.
Every story is alive.
Twenty winters in Tampa
have pulled lines
all over his face.

There are pictures taken.
My grandmother holds her only son,
as if a black trunk somewhere
were trying to pull him in.

11
He never married.
Working at Lakey's Foundry
in Muskegon,
he fell in love with Mary.
Before the carnie life
filled his body
they danced, went to movies.
Then, she fell away and married.
At the Paw Paw fair my uncle
sold hot dogs wrapped in dough,
thought of the long picnics in
Grand Rapids,
the beautiful girl
who wanted more than a life
of hot trailers,
a nightly walk through the
freak show.

12
The only thing he ever wanted to do,
he's doing.
Still, at Thanksgiving,
the family will mutter
about "crazy Stuart," "carnie,"
waiting for the big break.
Somewhere inside,
perhaps a long bone of my leg,
he is dancing,
his hands and arms are worn smooth,
used constantly like good tools.

Barbara Drake was born in Abilene, Kansas in 1939, and now lives in Okemos with her writer husband Al Drake. She edits Stone Press publications and also teaches writing and women's studies at Michigan State University. Her work has appeared in *Transpacific, Epoch, Sumac* and other magazines, and Stone Press recently published her *Field Poems* (1975).

Photo by Bud Drake

Good Friends and First Impressions

"I got a sunburn on my ass today," you said,
and flipping your tennis skirt
like an east coast can-can girl
you gave the party a peek. It *was* red.

If I hadn't known you better I'd have thought,
Uh, uh, look out for that one.
But I don't think that way any more.

At another party, ten years ago at least,
when I met you the first time,
you reminded me of a Captain Easy lady.
Your legs were curvy
the way they looked in comic strips in 1940.
You looked energetic enough
to jump aboard a passing Chinese junk
or wave from the deck of an aircraft carrier
at Easy flying by.

But you'd a baby in the car, and we were all
too poor to be adventurers. "Women don't like me,"
you said. "Too much hair and lipstick."
But I liked you a lot. I'd see you pass our house
with the plaid stamp buggy full of bags and the baby.
You'd walk reading a *Vogue* or *Cosmopolitan,* such
other-than-grad-school-worldly stuff, with a pint
of Ripple, red or white, in a paper sack—
you'd take a sip, push the buggy a few steps
and read of Jackie, whom someone told you
you resembled. Giving the baby a slice
of Wonder bread white as an angel, you'd stop,
offer me a snort from the bottle.
You've always been one of my most generous
and unsanitary friends.

Well, that's how you looked to me then.
Also, behind the hedge in your yard painting

enormous self-portraits: I thought
you were trying to find your own face
when all the rest of us dealt in words.
Or you, pulling something from a wrinkled
Goodwill sack and saying in your New England voice
that sounded foreign on our West Coast,
"I found this lovely gown today."

In the hospital, after my daughter was born
and I lay like a tube of toothpaste someone
had squeezed flat, you came
bringing your odds and ends of lotions,
lipstick, perfume, the kimona of rose-colored silk
to bring me back to life.

And you laughing heartily, and you in tears,
and you seeing whatever you have seen of me,
and now after ten years and moving with husbands
and children and dogs and rooms full of furnishings
thousands of miles we are: here again, in the same town,
turning up at the same parties, knowing
too many of each other's secrets to ever talk
at parties about anything but these
true and untrue first impressions.

Magic Children

My children, you grow so,
you make me feel like a joke,
a tiny car a lot of clowns
climb out of.

How you multiply,
from none to three.
Your father and I must be
an old vaudeville act,
and life is quicker than the eye.

Rabbits, red and yellow scarves,
fountains of paper flowers
spring from you.
Doves disappear
in velvet curtains
of your hair.

Oh, my magic children—
you saw me in two,
are my bed of nails,
the burning coals I walk through,
proof against wounds.

Loves, how shall I tell you
what I feel?
Like fans of cards,
eternal and unreal,
we must all fold back
into our own illusions.

She Dreams Herself Titanic

She dreams herself titanic
like the boat
that could not sink
but did not float,
and in her ears
what he lusts for,
crystal chandeliers.

Again the jewelled
iceberg tears,
again the waters pour,
again the voice of ice,
I'll ride you
to the velvet floor.
She wakes at dawn,
nine hundred miles from shore,
submerged and calm.

Old Folk Tale

One night
as I lay by my husband and he
was asleep
I heard a voice cry,
Rapunzel, Rapunzel,
let down your golden hair.

I rose and went to the window
and there far below was a man
in a fancy dress suit
of crimson and jet velvet.

Now my own hair is short and black
so I threw him the end
of the bedspread (yellow chenille),
and hand over hand he climbed
until I could smell his breath
like creme de menthe
and hear the jingle of his spurs.

You're imagining this,
I told myself, so
just as his hand crept over the sill,
Rapunzel, that damned
little whore is dead,
I whispered, take me!

But he dropped to his horse
like an old movie cowboy
and fled.

The Ancestors

In those days
we lived in a cave.
We scraped the walls
pursuing fleas.
Our monkey feet
pattered down halls
blue as arteries.
We lit fires
and learned burning.
We killed a lot,
sometimes each other.
We knew only that self
ends at the skin,
and continual hunger.
Our children
grew up and up
until they were out
of sight.
We never let
our neighbors in.
Now, covered with vines,
we breathe as little
as possible;
no one believes
we are still alive.

Case History

My hands get all the abuse.
I'm sorry for them.
To begin with, there's a prophecy
of arthritis in my left thumb,
a new cut, crater-like,
in the joint of that,
and a scar inside on the right
points to the wrist.
Allergy creeps between fingers
blurring their definition.
A scar on my left index finger
from babysitting and slicing ham
badly, at thirteen, a crook
in a little finger (right) broken
playing volleyball at fifteen,
pencil lead scar on the palm
(grabbing to get the pencil back
from a boy in math, at sixteen),
cat scratch, veins, disinfectant
burns, hypo stains, carbon, ink,
freckles, indentation of a
wedding ring, light brown hair
that doesn't soften any blows,
life-line that used to be a stream
with many tributaries, now a canyon,
overall worn appearance and much more.
The rest of me is a child compared
to these hands, hands like a woman
with many children.

The Woman Gets Restless

The woman gets restless
as the supper on the stove
is nearing completion.
Her fork tests a potato,
breaks a bit of meat,
salts the green vegetable.
Before the set but unsurrounded table
she stands in an empty house
listening for the sound of a car.
Whoever you are,
if you come at this time
she will feed you.

Stuart Dybek, born in Chicago in 1942, has published poems in several literary magazines including *The Paris Review* and *Poetry Now*. Although he is currently teaching at Western Michigan University, he has held numerous other jobs including helicopter-washing and ice cream making, and he claims that "wrecking houses was the most fun."

Photo by David Diny

Lazarus

Returned to life
in perfect health,
as if death was the remedy
for terminal illness;
so if my wife is reluctant
to sleep with me
who can blame her?
A man mounts the stairs:
A black suit, make-up
still caked to his face,
a rosary braided
through his fist . . .
But she'll get over it.
The kids will bring their friends
home again after school,
and the dog stop howling.

And if they're not satisfied
the ring around the tub
is only dirt,
there now are options
(perhaps a new life
must be different).
Lawyers stand in my shadow,
life insurance tied up in court;
I'm on the circuit
with faith healers and kooks
who claim flying saucers
took them to Jupiter. We lounge
aboard yachts of aging millionaires,
while ghost writers bid for my
Adventures From Beyond.

Contracts, agents, endorsements, movies . . .
My style's a cryptic smile
as if there's plenty I could say
if they just got me drunk enough.

And the ladies flirt
like girls around a priest.
I tell them I'm just your average
working stiff.
Everything's funny, I answer
when they ask me on TV, "Mr. Lazarus,
why are you always smiling?"
Thanks for everything. Yes,
it's fine to be alive,
in love with myself again,
the next death my only worry.

Flight

It happens in one of the usual ways. I'm
running hurdles and with each hurdle stay airborne
longer till I'm rounding the track, but no longer
touching down. We go to her place and turn on
some Latin music, mix up rum & cokes with slices
of lime. I'm telling her how happy I am when I
fly, that it's the best feeling I know, and, of
course, she says "Teach me." So we start to dance,
whirling around the room and pretty soon our feet
are touching the walls, not the carpet. When I
let her go she floats back down slowly to the couch
and as her skirt and slip swirl up to the tops of
her nylons I notice she has the dark delicate legs
a friend once called "Spanish legs." The same
friend once referred to a certain woman's "dark
madrigal beauty." These are phrases I've never
forgotten no matter what state of mind. And now
I'm gliding with extended arms across the ceiling,
out the window where only a dim streetlight burns,
and for the first time suddenly realize it's towards
death. There's no immediate danger such as falling.
It's that the direction one must go in order to fly,
to possess this unnatural power, is death. But
flight has always meant I'm happy, I insist to myself,
has always meant that everything's alright. Too late.
Had I never tried to teach, I would have never had
to learn.

The Poems of the Condemned Man

The poems of the condemned man
lacked craftsmanship
but were sincere,
the critic remarked

as the warden
read them for reporters
just after the execution.

He said they reminded him
of the art of inmates of mental institutions,
those distorted canvases
he'd often admired
in his friend, the psychiatrist's private study,

or the watercolors
the President receives at Xmas
from armless soldiers
who have learned
to hold the paintbrush with their teeth.

In the Basement

For years he'd been throwing things down the stairs
into the basement.
He was always going to go down and arrange them.
Things: junk, crap, fragments like

innertubes
phillips screw drivers, putty knives, glass cutters, other
tools

2 x 4's
newspapers and magazines like National Geographic he might
want to reread someday
good boxes, bags, string
clothes for rags
nuts, bolts, nails, screws, washers that might come in handy
broken things: clocks, toasters, radios, flashlights
he was going to fix
you name it, it was in the basement

His wife, Wanda, would ask him, Arnie, where's the squeezer?
This lemon juice is getting in my cut.
It's in the basement.
In the basement! Well, goddamn, everything's always in
the basement around here. You said you were gonna fix it.

So he'd get up and walk down the hallway and slip the
chain off the door
unbolt the lock
turn the skeleton key
But when he'd look down the steep stairs into the dark,
inhaling that must, he'd feel weak—like a little boy.
He'd remember the years of standing there flinging
down everything that got in the way.
Things he hated

like Wanda's fuzzy slippers that made her legs look like
an old lady's

his kid's toys when they were left lying around
the chipped and broken things he knew he could never
repair

All down the stairs, waiting in a pile, rising
like dirty water, demanding that one day he must finally
brick up the door.
Brick up the little black paned windows in the backyard
behind the weeds,
Having to tell potential buyers: Basement? No, there's
no basement here. This house never had a basement. The furnace?
Oh, we keep that in the attic.

Night of Voyeurs

It's more than silhouettes tonight,
every window in the city lit,
shades lifted, curtains open.
As one suspected, the dark buildings
full of lovers, undressing
beneath lightbulbs, before mirrors,
men & women, men & men, women & women, embracing.
Even the loners visible, flickered
by single candles, touching
places they've usually chosen to keep secret.
So much nakedness!
And the streets empty
except for newsboys moving through shadows,
leafless trees snatching underclothes
out of wind, the El clattering
above the roofs
like a strip of blue movie.

Vivaldi

When I met Vivaldi it was dark,
a ragman lashed his horse's bells,
streets tilted into slow wind-tunnels,

no, it was another night, in winter,
snow as soft as opium, two winos wassailed
down an alley through a milk truck's ruts,

in the subways a violin was whistling
down chrome tracks, past cobalt semaphores,
rats and pennies underneath the 3rd rail . . .

Has it ever been so quiet that you've heard
the manhole covers rumble when the El goes overhead?
Icicles growing? Could tell the difference
between the sound of filaments in lightbulbs
burning down, and a dulcimer played in a padded cell?

A meager music hovers everywhere:
at mouths of drains, echoing stairwells
where girls in muslin disappear
whispering "allegro."

When I closed my eyes,
less than a ghost,
Vivaldi cupped a mouth-harp
like a match against the wind.

Hugh Fox was born in Chicago in 1932. He is editor of *Ghost Dance: The International Quarterly of Experimental Poetry* and the author or editor of numerous collections of poetry and criticism. Some recent books include *The Gods of Cataclysm* (1975) and *The Face of Guy Lombardo* (1976). *Through the Smoking Mirror,* a collection of South American Indian poetry is forthcoming. He teaches in the Department of American Thought and Language at Michigan State University.

Photo by Nona Fox

"Christ, that was a real one," he said

"Christ, that was a real one," he said after he'd gotten
his breath back from the slap of the last wave that had curled
around the whole boat, would have sunk them if most of the boat
hadn't been enclosed—except for the wheel-spot which he'd
left open except for a windshield. More sporting, "in touch
with the elements."

She was gone. Not a trace of her. Not a cry, a hand, a
struggle, a whimper, a breath, a hair left. And inside the cabin
the baby, strapped in the car-seat they'd rigged up for her,
started to wail and wail and wail.

He got the boat in, anchored, got himself and the baby
to land, into the car, soaked, cold, back to the farm.

Get into some dry clothes,
            Feed the baby,
        then call the Coast Guard,
            report the death.

He wasn't really there. He was humbly trapped inside someone
else's body, watching the slow dumb unravelling of someone else's
life.

In the front door. He could see straight through into the
bedroom, she was there waiting for the baby, walked in, handed
the baby down into her cold, white, wet, bloodless arms.

His reaction to her asking for a divorce

His reaction to her asking for a divorce was so surprisingly
bland, even empathetic . . . generous, that it depressed her.

"Let's talk about it," he suggested. Out on to the grounds,
he went over to the control-box for the electric fence, "I turned
it off, I know how you hate it."

Even the idea of it. If you have so much that most of
your energy goes into ringing yourself around with protection
to keep out the rest of the world, then it hardly seems worth it.

"Why . . . ?"

It was sunny, windy, all banana leaves and eucalyptus and
palms, a sprinkler slowly nodding back and forth on the lawn
up ahead, but there was the fence around it all, you could always
peep around a corner, walk ten steps and see the fence.

"Why go into it *again*," she said, "they're such submicro-
scopic things, feelings . . . I miss Out There."

It was chilly, she wanted to go inside.

He grabbed the sprinkler, screwed off the sprinkler-head,
put his thumb over the nozzle, "Come on, let's have the facts,"
he said, playing, sprinkling her, getting her all wet.

"It's too cold," she said, "come on. . . . "

Wouldn't really have minded if he could really play,
let go . . . ever. . . .

"Come on, you're getting me drenched," she said, getting
oddly afraid now, "I'm going to go change clothes."

Sprayed the water right on her now, advanced on her, heavy,
staring, intense, fucking creep,

"What are you doing, for crissake," soaked, drenched, forcing
her back, then dropped the hose, pushed her back against the
fence, a sound like paper tearing, he stood over her, checked to
be sure. He wasn't quite sure what to do now, turn the juice
back down, leave it up, error, error, error, it was just a
question of finding the most plausible context.

The swing in the willow swung out

The swing in the willow swung out over the pond. Her daughter
couldn't swim, she almost cut the ropes through and when they
    broke
and she fell in the water and almost made it to shore she put her
foot on her daughter's head—careful, careful not to touch her
face—and held her under.

Six weeks on the road. He came in, the house seemed deserted.
Incense coming from upstairs. He opened the bedroom door, she was
sitting in the bed propped up, surrounded by pillows, all pink and
gold and perfect, and it wasn't until he'd touched her cold face
that he saw that the eyes weren't really inside the eye-sockets,
that there were other lips under her lips saying,

"Won't I do now?"

She was always knitting, weaving

She was always knitting, weaving, wore long knitted
wool skirts and sweaters, shawls, she was always warm, soft,
woolly . . . and when she died she was almost finished with a rich
brown, russet, umber, burnt Sienna afghan which her husband
took in his arms and held against his face and then folded
up and put on the sofa and every evening after dinner he'd
stretch out on the sofa with the afghan over him and take a
short nap.

Seven months later he remarried and one evening when he
went to take his short after-dinner nap he woke up dreaming
he was covered with tentacles all lined with powerful suckers,
the afghan tight over his face, corded around his neck.

As he folded it up in a cardboard storage box and put
it in the attic, he began to become aware of all things in

the house that she had knitted or woven, blankets, pillow-
covers, ties, sweaters, caps, mufflers, other afghans,
shawls, even the rugs in the dining room and the big bedroom
upstairs.

There was something white sticking out of the sand

There was something white sticking out of the sand. Thinking
it was a shell he stopped, dug around it. It was bone, pulled it
out of the sand . . . a human femur.

"It hasn't been that many years since the second world war."

He looked up surprised. He hadn't seen her. A native girl,
25, 26 . . .

"I didn't see you."

"I work at the hotel. It's my day off," she said.

"So you think it's some second world war soldier's bone," he
said, holding it in his hand, yellowed, aged, weathered, like
a piece of old yellow plastic.

"There were a lot of natives killed too," she said, "you never
know."

He threw it into the water, as far as he could. And kept
walking. She tagged along with him.

"How long have you been here?" she asked.

"A week, another week to go. I'm from New York, just left
the whole thing behind . . . ," he said, not mentioning his wife
and two children. Prelude to divorce. Preliminary cracking.

"And you like it here?"

"Except for the mosquitos and the prehistoric cockroaches, great . . . "

. . . . . .

On the edge of dusk now. She'd been a little too easy. He didn't know if she wanted money or not. Christ, from Captain Cook to now, talk about the Fall from Innocence. He opened his eyes, turned to talk to her. She wasn't there and when he tried to call out, his voice emerged not like a voice at all but a high-pitched, penetrating squeal, like rabbits screaming, carried off screaming by owls.

from Apotheosis of Olde Towne

1

Dress goods,
Silk,
Cloaks,
Shawls,
Flannels,
Embroideries,
Kid gloves,
The city was always based on trade, and the mahogany
butterflies throwing their incense into the eyes of
orphans huddled on the corner of Schiller and Wells,
creak for want of exercise.

. . .

3

Al Capone sitting in the first row crying
over Sierra's THE KINGDOM OF GOD,
with autographed ($10,000 an autograph)
portraits of Washington,
Lincoln
and William Hale Thompson in his
wallet, hears a
twig crack in the sixth
row and drops to the floor
as Old (odd) Al Parson
starts throwing dynamite around
like roses.

. . .

5

THE EIGHT FOOT POWHATAN HAND-
CARVED OUT OF SOLID MAPLE THAT

STOOD ON THE CORNER OF TWENTY-
SECOND STREET AND WABASH AVENUE
IN FRONT OF JOE GEDDY'S PLACE,
TOGETHER WITH THE MEZZOTINT
POCAHONTAS (carved by the same hand)
THAT STOOD ON THE NORTHEAST
CORNER OF CHICAGO AND CLARK,
AND OTHER VARIOUS AND SUNDRY
INDIANS CARVED BY WALTER
CAMPBELL

    SHALL BE RESURRECTED

      . . .

12

Consider
clocks, pots, kiosks, pools, bollards, ramps,
drains, grids, fountains and. . . .

the naked young girl, on the
    ball of one foot leaping
    upward, smoothes her hair
    a moment, dallies with time,
    and disappears. . . .

Dan Gerber (b. 1940) has published two collections of poems, *The Revenant* (1971) and *Departure* (1973), and two novels, *American Atlas* (1973) and *Out of Control* (1974). He has written articles for *New York, Playboy,* and *Sports Illustrated* and is currently at work on two nonfiction books. Originally from Grand Rapids, he lives near Fremont "on the Amazing X Ranch with five dogs, five cats, two horses and an ass named Maria."

The Russian Poem II

We are children grown strange
sleeping on airplanes
in cities on farms

I'm the last poet of country roads
but there'll always be another
The wind will take up my singing
the snow covers my tracks
when life grows impatient
and stalks from the room like a spoiled child

Here I am watching the snow
coat the golden domes of cathedrals
falling five thousand miles from home
where the apples are barely ripe
I've come to Moscow to justify
the Russian names I would write
and have written
I walk by the river
and through Red Square
        lights dramatic on the Kremlin wall
reader of too much Yesenin and Mayakovsky
But this isn't my country   It isn't Christmas
I can't live in this play I've contrived

I want a burger and shake

The Russian Poem IV

From my windows on Brodsky Street
the last yellow leaves
at last at ease a human place
cold Autumn on Nevsky Prospect
the Winter Palace
the Neva spread out like Venice
columns of St. Issac's
lapis and malachite
colors of perpetual Earth
and across the square a broken window
balcony where Yesenin hung himself
    Isadora laughing in Paris
Dostoevsky Pushkin Gogol Gorky
globes of a streetlamp
a little rain
somewhere through walls a violin tuning
voices drift from the street
I've slept away the afternoon

Grey Moscow's another world
    the collective mind hums
The woman in the window reads Henry Miller
looks down at the street
and smiles

Home From Russia

Season of Calypso
Winter and the solitary leaf
I've just returned from Moscow
While I was away leaves fell
and another dark November
    It has all happened before
and at this moment in Leningrad
a taxi
rumbles through almost empty streets
Night has fallen   the rain stopped
I slam the door of the cab
My shoes skim over the glistening pavement
trying to catch me

Homecoming

You return home
to find your house no longer there
The trees have grown back
and the toe of a boot you received for Christmas
protrudes through the loam of your floor
The door you locked in the morning
is the space between twilight
and the serialized stars
and your wife and children
their wings extended
circle the treetops
and sing indifferently of what you were

Death and the Pineapple

The fruit itself a giant pinecone
texture of an apple   the taste
an apple flavored with pine
If I died I couldn't eat pineapples
couldn't slice them with a large knife
or say the word that conjures the taste
pie-napple   pine-apple
couldn't run my hands
down the rough sides
or over the bushy top
let its juice drizzle down my chin
or wipe it away
with the back of my hand
rub it in my hair   gargle it
ponder the origin of its name
throw it at a strange and beautiful
woman on the rue Saint-Jacques
imagine a trip to Hawaii

The pineapple
is what we give up when we die
along with strawberries   coffee and sun
The room hovers about me
one more skull
the trees around the house
the sky around the trees
the stars around the sky
How could I escape so many enclosures
what would I see
what tastes   what sins
and if existence exists in space
what space   I can't imagine nothing

A house I once visited
had a pineapple over the door
a pineapple over the newel post
a pineapple in the center of the table

Surely these people had lived
They said it was their family crest
It's my family crest
my sign   my life
a galaxy of pineapples

I considered all the pineapples
growing under the sun
and will enjoy the good of my labor
all the days of my pineapple
for there is a wicked man
who prolongeth his pineapple
in his wickedness
and not a just man on earth
that doeth good and sinneth not

Journal Entry: April 5, 1974

Dan Gerber 1898–1974

Though supposedly Spring
snow is falling for the third straight day

Two weeks ago my father died
and I'm with him now
more than when he was living
I see him with my ancestors
thinner
in a white linen suit and Panama hat
He dances with my mother
or stands in the back of a Model T truck
in his uniform   just back from France

Then sitting on his knee
unjustly spanked
my lips protrude and my chin
forms a cauliflower of rage

I follow him like an old black dog
Yabut   he calls me
Yeh, but   I say   *but it isn't fair*

I feel the cold
through the soles of my shoes
the peepers sing from the pond
a few more flakes in the air

Nocturnes I

As sleep comes I imagine I'm a carpenter
resting from nails from the rhythmic hammer
from the saw and whisper *death death death*
fitting and joining with well made tools
pressed to sleep with darkness and the words
'tomorrow I will *do* something   tomorrow I will *make* something
and tomorrow tomorrow
silent as catsleep and the angel of thieves

Two Clouds

These songs
may be known
without singing

Five black crows
who steal corn

A pine forest
surrounding
individual trees

A power line leading
to an empty field

One brown apple
sweet beyond tasting

Two clouds
that pass only for clouds

Yellow

It is of daffodils
and dandelions
bananas and the dust
screening the sun
where it gathers
the earth
Yellow has been a long time
It would be
a world without salt
without it
It is your hair
and the way I feel these mornings
It is autumn
and that dress
worn for the first time

Donald Hall (b. 1928), a native of Connecticut, came to Michigan in 1957 to teach at the University of Michigan in Ann Arbor. He has published more than thirty books all told, including prose, juveniles, anthologies, and editions. His six books of poems include *Exiles and Marriages* (1955), *The Dark Houses* (1958), *A Roof of Tiger Lilies* (1964), *The Alligator Bride* (1969), *The Yellow Room* (1971), and *The Town of Hill* (1975). His prose work includes *String Too Short to be Saved* (1961), *Henry Moore* (1966), and *Writing Well* (1976). He is also author of a forthcoming biography of Dock Ellis tentatively titled *Getting Down and Staying Up*.

Kicking the Leaves

1.

Kicking the leaves, October, as we walk home together
from the game, in Ann Arbor,
on a day the color of soot, rain in the air;
I kick at the leaves of maples,
reds of seventy different shades, yellow
like old paper; and poplar leaves, fragile and pale;
and elm leaves, flags of a doomed race.
I kick at the leaves, making a sound I remember
as the leaves swirl upward from my boot,
and flutter; and I remember
Octobers walking to school in Connecticut,
wearing corduroy knickers that swished
with a sound like leaves; and a Sunday buying
a cup of cider at a roadside stand
on a dirt road in New Hampshire; and kicking the leaves,
autumn 1955 in Massachusetts, knowing
my father would die when the leaves were gone.

2.

Each fall in New Hampshire, on the farm
where my mother grew up, a girl in the country,
my grandfather and grandmother
finished the autumn work, taking the last vegetables in
from the cold fields, canning, storing roots and apples
in the cellar under the kitchen. Then my grandfather
raked leaves against the house
as the final chore of autumn.
One November I drove up from college to see them.
We pulled big rakes, as we did when we hayed in summer,
pulling the leaves against the granite foundation
around the house, on every side of the house,
and then, to keep them in place, we cut pine boughs
and laid them across the leaves,
green on red, until the house
was tucked up, ready for snow
that would freeze the leaves in tight, like a stiff skirt.

Then we puffed through the shed door,
taking off boots and overcoats, slapping our hands,
and ate in the kitchen, rocking, and drank
black coffee my grandmother made,
three of us sitting together, silent, in gray November.

3.
One Saturday when I was little, before the war,
my father came home at noon, from his half day at the office,
and wore his Bates sweater, black on red,
with the crossed hockey sticks on it, and raked beside me
in the back yard, and tumbled in the leaves with me,
laughing, and carried me, laughing, my hair full of leaves,
to the kitchen window
where my mother could see us, and smile, and motion
to set me down, afraid I would fall and be hurt.

4.
Kicking the leaves today, as we walk home together
from the game, among crowds of people
with their bright pennants, as many and bright as leaves,
my daughter's hair is the red-yellow color
of birch leaves, and she is tall like a birch,
growing up, fifteen, growing older; and my son
flamboyant as maple, twenty,
visits from college, and walks ahead of us, his step
springing, impatient to travel
the woods of the earth. Now I watch them
from a pile of leaves beside this clapboard house
in Ann Arbor, across from the school
where they learned to read,
as their shapes grow small with distance, waving,
and I know that I
diminish, not them, as I go first
into the leaves, taking
the step they will follow, Octobers and years from now.

5.
This year the poems came back, when the leaves fell.
Kicking the leaves, I heard the leaves tell stories,
remembering, and therefore looking ahead,
and building the house of dying. I looked up
into the maples, and found them, the vowels of bright desire.
I thought they had gone forever.
I love you, I love you sang the bird, shaking
its black head from side to side, and its red eye
with no lid,
and its yellow beak, until six years of winter
cold—no pale April, no summer green, no brilliant October—
buried the bird under the yew tree.

6.
Kicking the leaves, I uncover the lids of graves.
My grandfather died at seventy-seven, in March
when the sap was running, and waits in a northern grave
where elms still drop their leaves;
and I think of my father again, dead twenty years,
coughing himself to death, at fifty-two, in the house
in the suburbs. Oh, how we flung
leaves in the air! How they tumbled and fluttered around us,
like slowly cascading water, when we walked together
in Hamden, before the war, when Johnson's Pond
had not surrendered to houses, the two of us
hand in hand, and in the wet air the smell of leaves
burning;
and in six years I will be fifty-two.

7.
Now I fall, now I leap and fall
to feel the leaves crush under my body, to feel my body
buoyant in the ocean of leaves, the night of them,
night heaving with death and leaves, rocking like the ocean.
Oh, this delicious falling into the arms of leaves,
into the soft laps of leaves!

Face down, I swim into the leaves, feathery,
breathing the acrid odor of maple, swooping
in long glides to the bottom of October,
where the farm lies curled against winter, and soup steams
its breath of onion and carrot
onto damp curtains and windows; and past the windows
the tall bare maple trunks and branches, the oak
with its few brown weathery remnant leaves,
and the pine trees, holding their green.
Now I leap and fall, exultant, recovering
from death, on account of death, in accord with the dead,
the smell and taste of leaves again,
and the pleasure, the only long pleasure, of taking a place
in the story of leaves.

Photographs of China

After the many courses, hot bowls of rice,
plates of pork, cabbage, duck, and peapods,
we return to Chia-Shun's living room,
to the fire and conversation.
                                Chia-Shun brings over
an old book of photographs, printed in France.
"I want to show you China," he says,
"our China. This river"—he spreads a page flat—
"my university was beside this river."
The river looks wide, in the sepia photograph,
maybe half a mile wide, geese floating on it, and junks.
Beyond the river, there are rolling darkening hills,
like elephant skin, like the brows of Indian elephants.

"During the war, we bathed ourselves in that river.
Oh, it was cold in the winter!"

*

Li Chi crosses the room, touching the furniture.
She sits on the sofa between us, and peers
into the pages of photographs, her glasses
nearly bumping the pages she turns.
"Here," she says, "is West Lake, which is my home.
I always lived near the water, until now,
in Ann Arbor." Her laugh makes a noise like paper.

"When I was first at the university, in China,
I lived so close to the water
that I could fish out my window!"
                                Later,
we will persuade her to sing a poem from T'ang
that she learned from her mother, in her mother's accents.

*

We sit on the sofa, turning the pages together.

When we come to the river again, the book lies flat,
and Chia-Shun says,
            "Thirty years ago, on Sundays
I would ask my friend to help me prepare my assignment.
Then I spent all day
walking alone in the mountains."
                        There were orange trees
beside the hot springs, even in frosty winter.

"How the gold shone in the green shadows then!"

*

"When I was teaching," Li Chi says, "in another city,
in 1941, the planes bombed the house where I lived.
Fortunately, I was not home at the time"—she laughs—
"but my clothes, *all* of my clothes,
were up in a tree."
            Chia-Shun laughs also,
and closes the book, and says,
"When I see these pictures, when I remember these things,"
—he looks like a boy, wild and pink with excitement—
"I want to live two hundred years!"
                        And Li Chi:
"When I close my eyes, because my eyes hurt me,
then it is West Lake that I see."

O Cheese

In the pantry the dear dense cheeses, Cheddars and harsh
Lancashires; Gorgonzola with its magnanimous manner;
the clipped speech of Roquefort; and a head of Stilton
that speaks in a sensuous riddling tongue like Druids.

O cheeses of gravity, cheeses of wistfulness, cheeses
that weep continually because they know they will die,
cheeses as blunt as gray rock,
cheeses of victory, cheeses wise in defeat.

Esrom as fundamental as a village family;
Pont l'Eveque intellectual, and quite well-informed; Emmenthaler
decent and loyal, a little deaf in the right ear;
and Brie the revealing experience, instantaneous and profound.

O cheeses that dance in the moonlight, cheeses
that mingle with sausages, cheeses of Stonehenge,
cheeses of the Pacific Ocean, cheeses of new grass,
cheeses with gold threads like the threads in tapestries.

Reblochon openly sexual; Bresse Bleu like music in October;
Caerphilly like pine trees, small at the timberline;
Port du Salut in love; and Caprice des Dieux
eloquent, tactful, like a thousand-year-old hostess.

O cheeses that are shy, that linger in the doorway,
eyes looking down, cheeses spectacular as fireworks,
cheeses of Lascaux, of bison carved in stone, cheeses
fat as a cushion, lolling in bed until noon.

Camembert distant and formal, then suddenly laughing;
Gruyère an old neighbor returned for a visit; Liederkranz
fresh and ebullient, jumping like a small dog, noisy;
and Dolcelatte, always generous to a fault.

O village of cheeses, I make you this poem of cheeses,
O family of cheeses, living together in pantries,
O cheeses that keep to your own nature, like a lucky couple,
this solitude, this energy, these bodies slowly dying.

Jim Harrison, "international white trash sports fop," was born in northern Michigan in 1937, and now lives on a farm near Leland where he writes poetry, fiction, and magazine articles. He has published four collections of poetry: *Plainsong* (1965), *Locations* (1968), *Outlyer and Ghazals* (1971), and *Letters to Yesenin* (1973). He has also published three novels, *Wolf* (1972), *A Good Day to Die* (1973), and *Farmer* (1976).

Letters to Yesenin

1

to D.G.

This matted and glossy photo of Yesenin
bought at a Leningrad newsstand—permanently
tilted on my desk: he doesn't stare at me
he stares at nothing; the difference between
a plane crash and a noose adds up to nothing.
And what can I do with heroes with my brain fixed
on so few of them? Again nothing. Regard his flat
magazine eyes with my half-cocked own, both
of us seeing nothing. In the vodka was nothing
and Isadora was nothing, the pistol waved
in New York was nothing, and that plank bridge
near your village home in Ryazan covered seven feet
of nothing, the clumsy noose that swung the tilted
body was nothing but a noose, a law of gravity
this seeking for the ground, a few feet of nothing
between shoes and the floor a light year away.
So this is a song of Yesenin's noose which came
to nothing, but did a good job as we say back home
where there's nothing but snow. But I stood under
your balcony in St. Petersburg, yes St. Petersburg!
a crazed tourist with so much nothing in my heart
it wanted to implode. And I walked down to the Neva
embankment with a fine sleet falling and there was
finally something, a great river vastly flowing, flat
as your eyes; something to marry to my nothing heart
other than the poems you hurled into nothing those
years before the articulate noose.

2

to Rose

I don't have any medals. I feel their lack
of weight on my chest. Years ago I was ambitious.

But now it is clear that nothing will happen.
All those poems that made me soar along a foot
from the ground are not so much forgotten as never
read in the first place. They rolled like moons
of light into a puddle and were drowned. Not even
the puddle can be located now. Yet I am encouraged
by the way you hung yourself, telling me that such
things don't matter. You, the fabulous poet of
Mother Russia. But still, even now, school girls
hold your dead heart, your poems, in their laps
on hot August afternoons by the river while they wait
for their boyfriends to get out of work or their
lovers to return from the army, their dead pets to
return to life again. To be called to supper. You
have a new life on their laps and can scent their
lavender scent, the cloud of hair that falls
over you, feel their feet trailing in the river,
or hidden in a purse walk the Neva again. Best of all
you are used badly like a bouquet of flowers to make
them shed their dresses in apartments. See those
steam pipes running along the ceiling. The rope.

8

I cleaned the granary dust off your photo with my shirtsleeve.
Now that we are tidy we can wait for the host to descend
presumably from the sky as that seems to exhaust the alternatives.
You had a nice summer in the granary. I was out there with you
every day in June and July writing one of the six week wonders,
another novel. Loud country music on the phonograph, wasps
and bees and birds and mice. The horses looked in the window
every hour or so, curious and rather stupid. Chief Joseph stared
down from the wall at both of us, a far nobler man than
we ever thought possible. We can't lead ourselves and he led
a thousand with a thousand horses a thousand miles. He was a god
and had three wives when one is usually more than enough for
a human. These past weeks I have been organizing myself into

my separate pieces. I have the limberness of a man twice my age
and this is as good a time as any to turn around. Joseph was
very understanding, incidentally, when the Cavalry shot so many
of the women and children. It was to be expected. Earth is
full of precedents. They hang around like underground trees
waiting for their chance. The fish swam for four years solid
in preparation for August the seventh, 1972, when I took his life
and ate his body. Just as we may see our own ghosts next to
us whose shapes we will someday flesh out. All of this suffering
to become a ghost. Yours held a rope, manila, straight from
the tropics. But we don't reduce such glories to a mudbath.
The ghost giggles at genuflections. You can't buy him a drink.
Out in a clearing in the woods the other day I got up on a
stump and did a little dance for mine. We know the most fright-
ening time is noon. The evidence says I'm half way there, such
wealth I can't give away, thirty four years of seconds.

9

What if I own more paper clips than I'll ever use in this
lifetime. My other possessions are shabby: the house half
painted, the car without a muffler, one dog with bad eyes
and the other dog a horny moron. Even the baby has a rash on
her neck but then we don't own humans. My good books were
stolen at parties long ago and two of the barn windows are
broken and the furnace is unreliable and field mice daily
feed on the wiring. But the new foal appears healthy though
unmanageable, crawling under the fence and chased by my wife
who is stricken by the flu, not to speak of my own body which
has long suffered the ravages of drink and various nervous
disorders which make me laugh and weep and caress my shotguns.
But paperclips. Rich in paperclips to sort my writings which
fill so many cartons under the bed. When I attach them I say
it's your job after all to keep this whole thing together. And
I used them once with a rubberband to fire holes into the
face of the president hanging on the office wall. We have freedom.
You couldn't do that to Brezhnev much less Stalin on whose

grave Mandelstam sits proudly in the form of the ultimate
crow, a peerless crow, a crow without comparison on earth.
But the paperclips are a small comfort like meeting someone
fatter than myself and we both wordlessly recognize the face
or meeting someone my age who is more of a drunk, more savaged
and hag ridden until they are no longer human and seeing
them on the street I wonder how their heads which are only
wounds balance at the top of their bodies. A manuscript of
a novel sits in front of me held together with twenty clips.
It is the paper equivalent of a duck and a company far away
has bought this perhaps beautiful duck and my time is free again.

17

Behind my back I have returned to life with much more surprise
than conviction. All of those months in the cold with neither
tears or appetite no matter that I was in Nairobi or Arush, Rome,
the fabled Paris flat and dry as a newsphoto. And lions looked
like lions in books. Only the rumbling sound of an elephant shooting
water into his stomach with a massive trunk made any sense. But I
thought you would have been pleased with the Galla women in Ethiopia
and walking the Colonnade near the Vendome I knew you had walked
there. Such a few signs of life. Life brings us down to earth he
thinks. Father of two at thirty-five can't seem to earn a living.
But whatever muse there is on earth is not concerned with groceries.
We like to believe that Getty couldn't buy a good line for a billion
dollars. When we first offered ourselves up to her when young and
in our waking dreams she promised nothing. Not certainly that we
could buy a bike for our daughter's birthday or eat good cuts of
beef instead of hamburger. She doesn't seem to care that our wine
is ordinary. She walks in and out the door without knocking. She takes
off her clothes and ruins the marriage bed. She out and killed
you Sergei for no reason I can think of. And you might want to
kill her but she changes so fast whether into a song, a deer, a pig,
the girl sitting on the pier in a short dress. You want to fish but
you turn and there larger than any movie are two thighs and louder
than any howl they beckon you to the life they hold so gently. We

said that her eyes were bees and ice glistened in her hair. And we
know she can become a rope but then you're never sure as all rope
tends to resemble itself though it is common for it to rest in coils
like snake. Or rope. But I must earn our living and can't think
about rope though I am to be allowed an occasional girl drawing up
her thighs on a pier. You might want her even in your ghostly form.

18

Thus the poet is a beached gypsy, the first porpoise to whom it
occurred to commit suicide. True, my friend, even porpoises have
learned your trick and for similar reasons: losing hundreds of
thousands of wives, sons, daughters, husbands to the tuna nets.
The seventh lover in a row disappears and it can't be endured.
There is some interesting evidence that Joplin was a porpoise and
simply decided to stop breathing at an unknown depth. Perhaps the
navy has her body and is exploring ways to turn it into a weapon.
Off Boca Grande a baby porpoise approached my boat. It was a girl
about the size of my two year old daughter who might for all I know
be a porpoise. Anyway she danced around the boat for an hour
while her mother kept a safer distance. I set the mother at ease by
singing my infamous theme song: "Death dupe dear dingle devil flower
bird dung girl," repeating seven times until the mother approached
and I leaned over the gunnel and we kissed. I was tempted to swim
off with them but remembered I had a date with someone who tripled
as a girl, cocaine dealer and duck though she chose to be the last,
alas, that evening. And as in all ancient stories I returned to the
spot but never found her or her little girl again. Even now mariners
passing the spot deep in the night can hear nothing. But enough
of porpoise love. And how they are known to beach themselves. I've
begun to doubt whether we ever would have been friends. Maybe. Not
that it's to the point—I know three one eyed poets like myself
but am close to none of them. These letters might have kept me
alive—something to do you know as opposed to the nothing you chose.
Loud yeses don't convince. Nietzsche said you were a rope dancer
before you were born. I say yes before breakfast but to the smell
of bacon. Wise souls move through the dark only one step at a time.

19

Naturally we would prefer seven epiphanies a day and an earth
not so apparently devoid of angels. We become very tired with
pretending we like to earn a living, with the ordinary objects and
events on our lives. What a beautiful toothbrush. How wonderful
to work overtime. What a nice cold we have to go with the cold
crabbed spring. How fun to have no money at all. This thin soup
tastes great. I'm learning something every morning from cheap wine
hangovers. These rejection slips are making me a bigger person.
The mailbox is always so empty let's paint it pink. It's good for
my soul that she prefers to screw another. Our cat's right eyeball
became ulcerated and had to be pulled but she's the same old cat.
I can't pay my taxes and will be sent to prison but it will probably
be a good experience. That rattlesnake striking at dog and daughter
was interesting. How it writhed beautifully with its head cut
off and dog and daughter were tugging at it. How purging to lose
our last twenty dollars in a crap game. Seven come eleven indeed.
But what grand songs you made out of an awful life though you had
no faith that less was more, that there was some golden splendor
in humiliation. After all those poems you were declared a coward
and a parasite. Mayakovsky hissed in public over your corpse and
work only to take his own life a little while later. Meanwhile
back in America Crane had his Guggenheim year and technically
jumped ship. Had he been seven hundred feet tall he would have been
OK. I suspect you would have been the kind of friends you both needed
so badly. So many husbands have little time for their homosexual
friends. But we should never imagine we love this daily plate of shit.
The horses in the yard bite and chase each other. I'll make a carol
of my dream: carried in a litter by lovely women, a 20 lb bag of
    cocaine,
angels shedding tunics in my path, all dead friends come to life again.

Robert Hayden, born in Detroit in 1913, is currently teaching at
the University of Michigan. A prolific author, his recent
collections of poetry are: *A Ballad of Remembrance* (1962), *Selected
Poems* (1968), *Words in the Mourning Time* (1971), *The Night
Blooming Cereus* (1972), and *An Angle of Ascent* (1975). He is also
poetry editor of the Baha'i quarterly, *World Order.* He has been
appointed poetry consultant to the Library of Congress for 1977.

Middle Passage

I.

Jesus, Estrella, Esperanza, Mercy:

Sails flashing to the wind like weapons,
sharks following the moans the fever and the dying;
horror the corposant and compass rose.

Middle Passage:
       voyage through death
               to life upon these shores.

"10 April 1800—
Blacks rebellious. Crew uneasy. Our linguist says
their moaning is a prayer for death,
ours and their own. Some try to starve themselves.
Lost three this morning leaped with crazy laughter
to the waiting sharks, sang as they went under."

Desire, Adventure, Tartar, Ann:

Standing to America, bringing home
black gold, black ivory, black seed.

       Deep in the festering hold thy father lies,
       of his bones New England pews are made,
       those are altar lights that were his eyes.

Jesus Saviour Pilot Me
Over Life's Tempestuous Sea

We pray that Thou wilt grant, O Lord,
safe passage to our vessels bringing
heathen souls unto Thy chastening.

Jesus Saviour

"8 bells. I cannot sleep, for I am sick
with fear, but writing eases fear a little
since still my eyes can see these words take shape
upon the page & so I write, as one
would turn to exorcism. 4 days scudding,
but now the sea is calm again. Misfortune
follows in our wake like sharks (our grinning
tutelary gods). Which one of us
has killed an albatross? A plague among
our blacks—Ophthalmia: blindness—& we
have jettisoned the blind to no avail.
It spreads, the terrifying sickness spreads.
Its claws have scratched sight from the Capt.'s eyes
& there is blindness in the fo'c'sle
& we must sail 3 weeks before we come
to port."

> *What port awaits us, Davy Jones'*
> *or home? I've heard of slavers drifting, drifting,*
> *playthings of wind and storm and chance, their crews*
> *gone blind, the jungle hatred*
> *crawling up on deck.*

Thou Who Walked On Galilee

"Deponent further sayeth *The Bella J*
left the Guinea Coast
with cargo of five hundred blacks and odd
for the barracoons of Florida:

"That there was hardly room 'tween-decks for half
the sweltering cattle stowed spoon-fashion there;
that some went mad of thirst and tore their flesh
and sucked the blood:

"That Crew and Captain lusted with the comeliest
of the savage girls kept naked in the cabins

that there was one they called The Guinea Rose
and they cast lots and fought to lie with her:

"That when the Bo's'n piped all hands, the flames
spreading from starboard already were beyond
control, the negroes howling and their chains
entangled with the flames:

"That the burning blacks could not be reached,
that the Crew abandoned ship,
leaving their shrieking negresses behind,
that the Captain perished drunken with the wenches:

"Further Deponent sayeth not."

Pilot Oh Pilot Me

II.

Aye, lad, and I have seen those factories,
Gambia, Rio Pongo, Calabar;
have watched the artful mongos baiting traps
of war wherein the victor and the vanquished

Were caught as prizes for our barracoons.
Have seen the nigger kings whose vanity
and greed turned wild black hides of Fellatah,
Mandingo, Ibo, Kru to gold for us.

And there was one—King Anthracite we named him—
fetish face beneath French parasols
of brass and orange velvet, impudent mouth
whose cups were carven skulls of enemies:

He'd honor us with drum and feast and conjo
and palm-oil-glistening wenches deft in love,

and for tin crowns that shone with paste,
red calico and German-silver trinkets

Would have the drums talk war and send
his warriors to burn the sleeping villages
and kill the sick and old and lead the young
in coffles to our factories.

Twenty years a trader, twenty years,
for there was wealth aplenty to be harvested
from those black fields, and I'd be trading still
but for the fevers melting down my bones.

    III.

Shuttles in the rocking loom of history,
the dark ships move, the dark ships move,
their bright ironical names
like jests of kindness on a murderer's mouth;
plough through thrashing glister toward
fata morgana's lucent melting shore,
weave toward New World littorals that are
mirage and myth and actual shore.

Voyage through death,
          voyage whose chartings are unlove.

A charnel stench, effluvium of living death
spreads outward from the hold,
where the living and the dead, the horribly dying,
lie interlocked, lie foul with blood and excrement.

> *Deep in the festering hold thy father lies,*
> *the corpse of mercy rots with him,*
> *rats eat love's rotten gelid eyes.*

> *But, oh, the living look at you*
> *with human eyes whose suffering accuses you,*

whose hatred reaches through the swill of dark
to strike you like a leper's claw.

You cannot stare that hatred down
or chain the fear that stalks the watches
and breathes on you its fetid scorching breath;
cannot kill the deep immortal human wish,
the timeless will.

"But for the storm that flung up barriers
of wind and wave, *The Amistad,* senores,
would have reached the port of Principe in two,
three days at most; but for the storm we should
have been prepared for what befell.
Swift as the puma's leap it came. There was
that interval of moonless calm filled only
with the water's and the rigging's usual sounds,
then sudden movement, blows and snarling cries
and they had fallen on us with machete
and marlinspike. It was as though the very
air, the night itself were striking us.
Exhausted by the rigors of the storm,
we were no match for them. Our men went down
before the murderous Africans. Our loyal
Celestino ran from below with gun
and lantern and I saw, before the cane-
knife's wounding flash, Cinquez,
that surly brute who calls himself a prince,
directing, urging on the ghastly work.
He hacked the poor mulatto down, and then
he turned on me. The decks were slippery
when daylight finally came. It sickens me
to think of what I saw, of how these apes
threw overboard the butchered bodies of
our men, true Christians all, like so much jetsam.
Enough, enough. The rest is quickly told:
Cinquez was forced to spare the two of us

you see to steer the ship to Africa,
and we like phantoms doomed to rove the sea
voyaged east by day and west by night,
deceiving them, hoping for rescue,
prisoners on our own vessel, till
at length we drifted to the shores of this
your land, America, where we were freed
from our unspeakable misery. Now we
demand, good sirs, the extradition of
Cinquez and his accomplices to La
Havana. And it distresses us to know
there are so many here who seem inclined
to justify the mutiny of these blacks.
We find it paradoxical indeed
that you whose wealth, whose tree of liberty
are rooted in the labor of your slaves
should suffer the august John Quincy Adams
to speak with so much passion of the right
of chattel slaves to kill their lawful masters
and with his Roman rhetoric weave a hero's
garland for Cinquez. I tell you that
we are determined to return to Cuba
with our slaves and there see justice done. Cinquez—
or let us say 'the Prince'—Cinquez shall die."

The deep immortal human wish,
the timeless will:

     Cinquez its deathless primaveral image,
     life that transfigures many lives.

Voyage through death
         to life upon these shores.

Conrad Hilberry (b. 1928) grew up outside of Detroit. Since 1962 he has taught at Kalamazoo College. His poems and criticism have appeared in many magazines including *Antaeus, Field, New Yorker,* and *Poetry Northwest.* His books include *Encounter on Burrows Hill* (1968), and *Rust* (1974).

Kalamazoo Gazette photo

For Katherine, 1952–1961

I

Your flesh is melted, I suppose,
To Indiana clay. Only your bones
Attend that deep box. Graceful
They must be, even now.

II

Dead as many years
As you lived. If a child
Grows back down, a year
For a year, you are a hard
Birth to be taken in,
A conception, and nothing.

III

Katharine, we die.
My father is dead
And his brother.
Some of us grow down
While we live.
          What? Am I telling you
About death?
          This is what I know:
You visited the neighbors'
Cats. In the park, you
Climbed down rocks
To fern and twisting
Water. Once we camped
By a soggy little lake, drove
Home in the rain, late,
Singing, the lights of the towns
Blurred and wonderful in the wet
Pavement. We planted
Corn, do you remember?

And in August felt
The full ears, husked
Them, broke the sweet
Kernels with our teeth.

You grew so easily
There seemed no other way.
Your voice held out
Its hands, palms up.

This motion, this poise—
Broken to wet bones in a box.

IV

On this day of your death,
We love. The steep
Water of your making
Is still green—
And will be, will be.
The fern, the falls,
The keeping on.

Sea

The sea breaks. I turn
And take it, a monk's
Hood over my head,
Then dive into a wave,
Feeling the heave and slough
As tangled water passes.

Out beyond breakers, water swells
And settles, taking a deep breath
For the landing. Buoyed by this depth
I let all sinews go, sell these bones
To the sea—two good shoulders
And a bad leg. Let water take

Them, salvage or discard them
As it will. No time but this.
No obligation, no comfort, no
Accomplishment. No person but
The sea with its cold hands. The sun,
Too far, touches no part of me.

Without my willing it, the sea
Brings from its hoard a salt recollection:
The bitter ache for a daughter
Dead, a girl who walked weightless
In my love. Her absence rises
And falls with me in the heavy water.

Shouts from the beach. Another girl,
Alive, runs to taste the cold
In a single dash and fall.
She swims out, and I crawl
Over the curl of breakers
Toward the lame and slippery shore.

Harry Houdini
The Hippodrome, New York, January 7, 1918

Jennie clomped on stage,
Ten thousand pounds they say
And you can well believe it,
Lumpy elephant standing
In those four wash buckets
Of feet. They opened
The cabinet, front and back,
And turned it to show us:
Empty right through.
Jennie walked around, then in.
Houdini raised his arms
Like a preacher
And fired his pistol.
When they drew the curtain,
Nothing. Ten thousand pounds
Vanished. Blue ribbon around her neck,
Alarm-clock wrist watch
On her left hind leg,
Gone.

I felt the Lord moving in me
The way He moved in Jennie,
His hand on my shoulder.
I shouted, "Praise God.
He is taking off my flesh.
I am like to fly. Praise the Lord."
My body vanishing, the flesh melting
Upward into the air.

But Houdini stopped it. "Go back
To your body," he said. "It is not yet
Judgment Day. Go back to your body,
Madame." And fired the foolish pistol again.
He couldn't stand a real miracle.
So I went back. Flesh in its sack of skin
Slung from my shoulders. Jennie was gone,

Ten thousand pounds, but he wouldn't let me
Shed my sackful.

       The room went heavy.
Arms, buttocks, breasts hung
Fat as sausages across the chairs.

Blind Girl on the Santa Fe

Not diverted by this windowful
of cows or the distant tractor like a pen stroke
changing the color of a field,
all day long you know the low hums,
old forms, the wordless, pitching voices of parents
or lovers, the weight of what has actually happened
pressing in like the close air of a tunnel.
All day long you know those presences
we speak to sometimes in the dark of the night.

The passing feast our senses treat us to
is what happens to be there, not what moves us.
If sense impressions were the whole of it,
the world were one long vanishing. In every
eye-blink, the gaudy sights are seen and gone.
But what occurs cannot be said to vanish.
Having passed, it turns to stubborn fact,
pressing itself on everything that is.

Our anger, fear, desire, hatred, hunger
rumble like yours out of the rods and axles
of this ancient rolling stock. Together
we stumble under our baggage and lurch
out the rear door through steam and bells
toward the strange hollow of the station.

Hunger

The goat hungers. Everything that lies
in his way, he devours. He crams
into himself a universe of grass,
shrubs, debris, and yesterday's
goats.

　　Yet everything remains.
Coming over the shoulder of the hill,
you see the uncut grass, the sumac, discarded
shirts and cereal boxes, just as they were,
and, tethered in place, the goat—

innumerable goats, all chewing.

Portholes

Suppose you could not turn away. Suppose
your vision ran around the corner, through
the wall, so that you never could ignore
my vacant eye, the hunch or swagger
of my shoulders. Suppose, while climbing dunes
beside Lake Michigan, you still could hear
the falter of my voice, telephoning
in the kitchen. Suppose the sweat
of molecules colliding in my bones
should rise as a sharp incense to your nose.
Suppose, in short, our senses told us
everything. Imagining that, we thank
our skins for having such poor portholes,
five small windows nudging our privacy
with a little local information. Our bodies
ration us our portion of the world.

Ignorant, we are tossed by breakers
that come dreaming up on our blind side;
our feet shuffle to some watery ragtime
we cannot hear. Still, may the slits
of our senses let in only what we need:
a few close words calling from skin to skin,
colors scrambling to each other's eyes,
the condiments of taste and smell
and finally touch, taking each other in.

David James was born in Detroit in 1955, and now lives in St. Clair Shores. He is a student at Western Michigan University where he edits *Currents*. His poems have appeared in *Poetry Now*, *Hiram Poetry Review*, and other magazines.

Photo by Joe Sgarlata

The Blind Man Who Sells Brushes

A blind man selling brushes
walks across the lawn, up the
front steps and knocks on your
door. From behind the living
room curtains you stare at his
white eyes rolling backwards
against his brain. The moment
you saw him coming you sent
the kids to the basement, shut
the windows, turned the radio off,
locked the front door. You figured
the blind man would just move on
to your neighbor's house. He drops
his black suitcase on the porch
and begins pounding on your screen.

The house is perfectly quiet.
Near dinnertime you bring the
children upstairs. Your husband
parks the car down the street
and sneaks up through the neighbors'
yards to the back door. The blind
man is smashing the screen with
his cane. The huge suitcase stuffed
with brushes falls off the porch
into the rose garden.

After dinner the family tiptoes
downstairs to watch TV without
the sound. Your husband taps his
foot to the beating of the blind
man who wants to sell brushes to
you. When it is late you join hands
and put your children to bed, fumbling
in the darkness. The blind man is
swinging at the doorknob with his cane.
Your husband climbs under the covers;

you lean over, pull your knees up,
breathing into his back.

In the morning the blind man's head
is screaming through your storm window.
You and the kids sit at the breakfast
table, heads bowed, praying;
O God, please let us kill him.

Tradition

My father brings whiskey home
from the steel mill after work.
Slivers of metal cut into his
eyes, reddened with pain; his
hair tangled with iron or pale
zinc. He drinks himself mad
every night, singing, pulling
his fist out of walls, through
picture windows. Mother kneels
in the backyard, praying.

Around here, traditions are kept
like wives. My father's way is
my way; nothing more. My life is
the bottle of whiskey he drinks,
the fist scarred with glass,
the reckless singing.

At dawn, he lifts himself from bed,
rinsing his crude face. Mother
struggles over breakfast. I wake up
to the shuffling of voices, the low
hiss of a skillet. It is 5:30 A.M.
The fog lies down outside our fence.
We go through the motions of eating
and then I watch my father,
crowding the sidewalk to the steel mill,
waste my life.

Making Yourself at Home

You open the front door with your good hand
and look in. There is plenty of room.
Sit down. Make yourself at home.

This is really more than you imagined.
Every room is in the right place;
the color of the walls matches your eyes.

There is bread in the oven, warm and fresh.
You sit at the table where knives and
forks and a plate have been put out.

This is where you'll sleep. The bed is soft
the way you like it. Larkspur is planted
outside the far window and you can watch it

come up in spring. You have no neighbors.
The land is flat for miles in all directions.
The grass turns under the ground at night.

Your body follows you through the house
doing exactly what you do. Tomorrow
you must teach it how to breathe.

Child Collecting

When your oldest son reaches
puberty, you tie him up and
shove him in a closet for a
couple years. It will all pass,
you say.

In the mornings when your other
kids run off to school and your
husband finally leaves for work,
you kneel down with your son,
stroking his hair for hours,
humming old nursery songs from
under your chest.

Often, when you open the door
you find him sucking on a coat
sleeve or pushing a hanger between
his legs. These things will all
work out for the best. You hand-feed
him yourself and then cuddle the
huge child on your lap, patting
his back.

The other children take turns
playing with him in the closet.
Neighbors casually say hello
when they hang up their coats,
commenting on how fine he looks.

When it is time for a younger child
to be put in the closet, you carefully
untie the rope and carry your son up
to his room, his mouth tearing at
your breast.

For Rent

The damp corners are filled
with children; crouched in,
hands tucked under. Their
warped eyes follow you around
the basement. Fungus breaks
from their faces like scales.

The landlady swings a broom
in the corner and they scatter
into crevices, behind shelves
and furniture. Shreds of clothes
cover the floor.

She says they come with the
lease, but are quite harmless.
You hear them move closer.
She turns out the light and
walks upstairs.

She gives you a pen to sign
the contract. When you do
the children rush into the room,
clawing at your legs like lepers,
squinting at your white hands.

Digging for Singapore

a small lumbertown in Michigan in 1860's
that was buried by the shifting sand dunes
of Lake Michigan

I.
The smell of fresh wood or lumbermen carving
their lives into the mouth of the Kalamazoo
River was all they had. Heavy axes littered
the front of the head cabin. One small man
balanced in the doorway with a cup of black
coffee rising in his face. He was ready
to dig.

And so were many other people. They knew
what was going to happen and wanted to dig.
Some had already packed up and moved to
Chicago, or worse, Benton Harbor. Still others
vowed to stay no matter what. This was all
they had.

The grandfathers would dig. The pretty girls
who stayed would bring the men cold water
to drink. Women would carry buckets of sand.
They would all dig. The grains sliced under
their fingernails; shovels broke in two like
twigs. One half-crazy lumberman took an axe
to a dune. His wife was having a child and
he couldn't move her.

The sand kept coming. The people kept digging
their homes. No one could pull Old Man Higgins
from the cabin when it collapsed. The sand
kept coming. Those who had wagons headed out.
Those who didn't, stood against their homes,
digging.

II.
The cracked dock inches out from the mountains
of sand. The tips of houses weasel up for air.
Two Cooper's hawks spiral above an old man who is
digging. His hands are threaded with slivers;
his face dented from cave-ins. He says he is
digging a home. I kneel beside him and start
digging for mine.

Janet Kauffman (b. 1945) grew up on a tobacco farm in
Pennsylvania and now lives on a farm near Hudson, Michigan.
Her work has appeared in several literary magazines including
The Beloit Poetry Journal, Poetry Now, and *The Ohio Journal.*

Photo by Beth Tinsler

Mennonite Farm Wife

She hung her laundry in the morning
before light and often in winter
by sunrise the sheets were ice.
They swung all day on the line,
creaking, never a flutter.
At dusk I'd watch her lift each one
like a field, the stretches of white
she carried easily as dream
to the house where she bent and folded
and stacked the flat squares.
I never doubted they thawed
perfectly dry, crisp,
the corners like thorn.

from **Tobacco**

Preface: Topping

We soaped our hands
with cold soap from a tin can,
then slipped into the rows.
We pulled tobacco suckers, snapped them down
broke off the pastel flowering tops, with slick fingers
feeling over each plant,
parting the green gumleaves,
steady as prophets who knew how to do things
effortlessly, hands taking charge,
blessing and breaking,
blessing, breaking.

1. Steamer on the Seedbed

Machines
like mothers pumping the beginning
every April on schedule,
spring steamed
out from under iron,
the metal lids lifting—
and there it was:
great gates opening,
whirring gears and camshafts
winging, the ungainly steamer
shaking wide bull flanks,
shimmering
heatwaves rising through unsteady air,
white clouds bursting into blue
and in the breeze the stinging
water spat off iron.

Somewhere inside the steamer's belly
roared fire.

2. Cultivating

On a two-seated cultivator, we sniffed exhaust,
inhaled blue clouds those long rose evenings;
leaning on a handle in each hand
we weaved around the stalks, furrowing
damp field into dark.
Doubled over and in the drug of it
I watched the velvet plants
with hair leaves moving untouched
below the tractor body, between harrows,
drifting like the blessèd on their way.
I let them go.

> *Tobacco's but an Indian weed,*
> *Grows green in the Morn, cut down at Eve . . .*

And now when I see in the shadow of porches
grey farm women
nodding to grey slippered feet,
I feel all over again the curve in my back,
the disproportionate torso
turned like a shell,
the vaginal hold on empty space
and that blue monoxide
cloud of summer we bent beneath to breathe.

3. Taking Down

A swinging trouble light sweeps through black
barn and cold. My father's breath the fog overhead
caught like a bush in the cone of low beam.
He walks on rails,
handing down tobacco, long leaves
flattened by the hang and like skins
stretched, veins dry.
We move mechanically under
huge roofed spaces,
among the hammered edges of machines—
tractors, harrows, plows hauled in,
the planter and the flatbed wagons.

Not hunters,
not driven,
we work and do without
the power to cast the shadow of iron,
even as the stun, the hush of arrow over snow—
that speeding dark—comes home.

Watercress

It was cold, and we gritted our teeth,
hands hooking under, cutting blind
in the black spring just out from rock.
Rooted to water, the tangle of green
we reached almost out of our reach
and carried back kettles of cress,
back through the orchard, the subdivision—
awkward, lucky as cooks
side-stepping soldiers, the slumped regiments—
with leaves pressing flat to our tongues
and a taste no remedy (no, not blood),
but the bite of a breaking
spring, its cold flows.

Rally

The Delta Ohio CycleRama just broke up a whole
hot afternoon, with Crazy Ed of course
leading the 200, Sunday spun behind him like braids.

I was out front in my striped green plastic
lounge chair, propped and dull.
I was thinking I had them, and I might have

had Kid Korman pulled in, gravel hailing the hedge,
and swung himself out of an ongoing cloud,
walking my way through the chicory stalks, mildly
asking lady got some gas (form-a-gasket, band-aid)
and I'd have said, take off your helmet sweetface
let me see your hair. Bright Baby Blue and Sugar Sal
I would have asked in, admired the gloves, boots, glitter
crashgear, and led them into shade and set out ice
and green mint tea in fine glasses
and said sweets we must do this more often.

The Volunteers

In the middle of the afternoon when people turn slowly
and never mind the smoke winds rolling,
the barn shingles snapped off all at once in flames.

The lid gone, everything flew out—hurrahs of fire
rocked the trees, and a small sun cooled.
The timbers of the peak bloomed full,

then fell; and in the slow of dreamers watching,
we saw a wheat field stretching out beyond,
a brushy line of woods, more sky.

—Well that's your barndance—easy enough
now to have a party with the volunteers,

their numbered hats, their slick coats heaped on grass.
They were young, excited by the whole thing

done with, the drifting smoke, the hay and metal stink.
They drank Crush and 7-Up and smiled.

Under the trees they spread their legs
and leaned on elbows, each one seeing the same

flame gone, water spent, and the sun
fired up again, wind in curl.

Jane Kenyon, born in Ann Arbor in 1947, still lives there, with her writer husband Donald Hall. Her work has appeared in many literary magazines including *American Poetry Review*, *The Ohio Review*, *The Nation*, and *The Paris Review*.

Cages

"Standing there they began to grow skins
dappled as trees . . . "
                            Jean Valentine

1

Driving to Winter Park, in Florida,
in March, with my husband,
past Cypress Gardens, and the baseball camps,
past the dead beagle in the road, his legs
outstretched—as if he meant to walk
on his side, in the next life.

At night, the air
smells like a cup of jasmine tea.
The night-bloomer, the white
flowering jasmine,
and groves of orange trees
breathing through their sweet skins.

And cattle in the back
of the truck, staggering
as the driver turns off the highway.

2

By the pool, here at the hotel,
animals in cages to amuse the guests:
monkeys, peacocks, a pair of black swans,
rabbits, parrots, cockatoos,
flamingoes holding themselves on one leg
perfectly still, as if they loathed
touching the ground.

The black swan floats
in three inches of foul water,
its bright bill thrust under its wing.

And the monkeys, one lying
in the arms of the other.
They look like Mary and Jesus
in the Pieta, one looking for fleas
or lice on the other, for succour
on the body of the other—
some particle of comfort, some
consolation for being in this life.

Now the smaller monkey gets down
from the other's lap.
He lunges across the cage
and pulls himself up the bars
until his face is level with mine.

3

He reaches through the cage
and grabs for my pen, as if
he had finally decided
to write a letter, long overdue.

I sit in the room for a long time,
a knot of paper in my fist.
Inside me a small animal
hardly breathing, frantic to get out.

Here in Florida,
in the baseball camps, the whole team
touches the palm of the player
who hits the home run. May it rub off
on me, may it rub off on me . . .
and hearing Jean read her poems
I feel ready to try again.

4

And the body, what about
the body? Sometimes it is
my favorite child, uncivilized
as those spider monkeys
with heart-shaped masks,
loose in the trees overhead.

They leap and cling
with their strong tails,
they steal food from the cages—
little bandits. If Chaucer
could see them, he would change
"lecherous as a sparrow"
to "lecherous as a monkey."
And sometimes my body
disgusts me. Filling and
emptying it disgusts me.

When I feel that way
I treat it like a goose
with its legs tied together,
stuffing it
until the liver is fat enough
to make a tin of paté. Then,

I agree with Bishop Cranmer
who called the body
"a cloud before the soul's eye."

his long struggle to be at home
in the body, this difficult friendship.

5

It's not easy to love a place
where people come to die,
where mortuaries advertise
on bus stop benches. And east of here,
the beaches, heaps of gutted
and broken shells. We sunbathe in a cemetery.

Still, I'm learning to love the world,
and this strange place, and sometimes even
the thrashing of my own heart
under my ribs,

and you, lying next to me
asleep or floating, breathing
in and out   in and out
through your sweet skin.

The Circle on the Grass

I

Last night the wind came into the yard,
and wrenched the biggest branch
from the box elder, and threw it down
—no, that was not what it wanted—
and kept on going.

This morning a man arrives
with ladders, ropes and saws,
to cut down what is left.

II

Eight years ago, someone
planted the sapling
mid-way between porch and fence,
and later that day,
looked down from the bedroom
on the highest branch.

The woman who stood at the window
could only imagine shade,
and the sound of leaves moving overhead,
like so many whispered conversations.

III

I keep busy in the house,
but I hear the high drone
of the saw, and the drop in pitch
as chain cuts into bark.

I clean with the vacuum
to obliterate the sound
until the man leaves for lunch.
Now the house is quiet
like a face paralyzed by strokes.

IV

All afternoon I hear the blunt
shudder of limbs striking the ground.
The tree drops its arms
like someone abandoning a conviction:
—perhaps I have been wrong all this time—

When it's over, there is nothing left
but a pale circle on the grass,
dark in the center, like an eye
that will not close.

The Suitor

We lie back to back. Curtains
lift and fall
like the chest of someone sleeping.
Wind moves the leaves of the box elder;
they show their light undersides,
turning all at once
like a school of fish.
Suddenly I understand that I am happy.
For months this feeling
has been coming closer,
making short visits, like a timid suitor.

At a Motel Near O'Hare Airport

I sit by the window all morning
watching the planes make final approaches.
Each of them gathers and steadies itself
like a horse clearing a jump.

I look up to see them pass,
so close I can see the rivets
on their bellies, and under their wings,
and at first I feel ashamed,
as if I had looked up a woman's skirt.

How beautiful that one is,
slim-bodied and delicate
as a fox, poised and intent
on stealing a chicken
from a farmyard.

And now a larger one, its
tail shaped like a whale's.
They call it sounding
when a whale dives,
and the tail comes out of the water
and flashes in the light
before going under.

Here comes a 747,
slower than the rest,
phenomenal; like some huge
basketball player
clearing space for himself
under the basket.

How wonderful to be that big
and to fly through the air,
and to make such a big shadow
in the parking lot of a motel.

Faye Kicknosway (b. 1936), a native of Detroit, writes poetry, fiction, and children's literature, and she is on the faculty of Wayne State University. Her poems have appeared in *The Paris Review*, *The Massachusetts Review*, and *The New York Quarterly*. She has published three books: *O You Can Walk On The Sky? Good!* (1972), *Poem Tree* (1973), and *A Man Is a Hook. Trouble.* (1974).

Photo by Sally Young-Chambers

Dear Editor:

this morning my paper arrived
different than usual. it was cut up
and pasted. it was illegible
and obscene. twenty-five people collapsed
in my doorway; some of them were the size

of cartoons and subscriptions. i chased them
all into the fireplace. they burned well
but smelled terrible. breakfast

should be a peaceful meal. coffee is bad
enough for the stomach without suicides, the size
of thumbs, floating in it. and crazy men, with guns,
popping out of the toaster, demanding parachutes
and money; i tell you,

mr. editor, it's more than a reader should bear. news
should be a distraction, like popcorn or cigars.
headlines should keep to their print, photographs
should not turn real. please

cancel my subscription. the tiny people in this
envelope are what remains of section b. they drowned
two nine yr old girls in my toilet, exploded
my cat and demanded political asylum of the spider
in the kitchen. i hope the trip to your desk
isn't too tiring for them; thinking
of what they'll do to you has been the only
bright spot in my day.

the cat

the cat
approaches and my life
discharges small green islands of meat
and blood, small blue faces knit
from the rags feeling can not absorb. the cat
approaches, licking the tiny pockets
of its grief. the cat
approaches, its winter arms burning,
its soft flesh burning. the cat
approaches and it is windows and photographs,
it is dwarves
coming loose from paintings, skin
coming loose from the heart. the cat
approaches and its fur is stiff and spiney and it chews
its whiskers with its leather teeth. the cat
approaches and its red hooves
dig my heart open. the cat
approaches and it is dust
rising from the nest of the universe
and i sleep
between its claws, blind
as salt, blind
as wood. the cat
approaches and its razor tongue
kisses the moon awake, kisses stars
loose from heaven. the cat
approaches and the earth, and the things of
the earth
yammer and yowl and drown in the thick sea
of its throat. the cat
approaches and the wind digs its hands into the mud
of my legs,
and feet
and i escape down
into the earth as roots and clay. the cat
approaches and dreams climb the chemic moisture
of its fur. the cat

approaches and its hearts noise, its wings
noise fits my body and my hands sweat,
my belly sweats and i

am the cat, moving
through the window of your dream, moving
through the earth of your dream,
the fire of your dream,
as blossoms and fingers,
as seaweed and hair,
as gemstones and apples; i

am the cat and i
move as moonlight,
as firelight,
as lamplight through
the thin red branches of your lips,
the thick green branches of your eyes.

this cat

this cat
is the length of my arm. its voice
comes over the telephone strange, distorted, from
the space only memory speaks. there is no way
to see inside it. it dreams

of food and carries its young
in spoons. its paws are hooves and its tail
is leather. and it speaks in a voice
swollen and red with tears. it has been
the bride of chance, of
optical illusion. the telephone

complains there isnt enough water
in what is said. and the cat nods, looking
at its wet, electric body. the telephone
bristles and the cat
bristles and the moon, out of reach in the bedroom wall,
dips her red fingernails into the cats
heart, into the telephones
heart, and i, caught in unsolved memories, hear
in their union a noise
like forks and knives
cutting up meat
on a plate.

He must be fat

He must be fat
and healthy and twelve years old.
He must be happy
and laughing and twelve years old.
Catch him. Beguile him. Catch
him. Tie him to a tree. He has entered
a sacred time.
Give him nine months of eating

the roots of the tree, the earth around
the tree. Give him nine
months of sitting in a cage
buried in the root of the river. Nine months is
the time of wax
coming to the body. Nine months is
the time of whiteness
coming to the eyes
of the body.
Kill him.
Send his head in a sack to his mother.
Bring sticks for the fire. Give her parts
of his body. Let her dip her fingers in, let her
lick her fingers as she cooks.
Twelve is a sacred age.
Bring cups
and bowls.

Oil trucks. The season of despair. Your grass

Oil trucks. The season of despair. Your grass
eyes watch from the moon.
You keep so much of the world out. Limit.
Dry heat, onions cooking, someone fifteen looking
at your legs. Bend nearer. Dry

throat. Someone knocking at your belly. At
the corner of your bed. Chicken feathers, angel
feathers, dust from the skin.
Strange names rise from your throat.
You walk the short space between houses, wondering
whom you seek. The cooking fire has gone

out. The old grandmother, chewing
at her fingers with her stumpy teeth, whines
'dust'

is her name. She sits
watching her body
disappear
down the rooster's throat.

the moon travels slow

the moon travels slow
with shopping bags
over its wrists
& its hat crooked
& its socks snagged
slow
weary
not even money for bus fare

when you plant cats in the ground

when you plant cats in the ground,
nothing grows.
not even peonies
or asparagus.
not even tulips
or peach trees.
nothing.
not even water
comes out of the ground.
or houses.
or children.
or anything useful.
not even if you
irrigate
or fertilize.
nothing.
not even if it rains.

not even if you learn spanish.
nothing grows.
and you can watch all you want.
and listen for the sound
of the new kittens under the ground
all you want.
even at night in your dreams.
but they wont crawl out.
they wont crawl out.
not even a thorn bush.
not even hollyhocks.

Philip Legler born in Dayton, Ohio, in 1928, now lives in Marquette, where he teaches at Northern Michigan University. In addition to numerous magazine publications, he has published two books of poems, *A Change of View* (1964) and *The Intruder* (1972). "I love living in the Upper Peninsula of Michigan," he says. "After 7 years here I even love the snow: what else can you do but give yourself up to it."

Photo by Leonard Hildreth

Sheet-Monger, Blanket-Hoarder

Sheet-monger, blanket-hoarder,
wool gatherer of nightmares,
wrapped in white linen like a corpse,
wrapped in your dreams, a straight-jacket,
I remember that night in Frisco
when we got our new bodies.
It wasn't an operation
performed by a team of specialists;
it wasn't a heart transplant;
nothing was sewn or grafted.
In our new bodies it was a miracle.

And all those years beaten by love,
strangled by love, crazy in the head for love,
you thought you were dying.
Your body, you were sure, was dead
like a person in trance, far away,
but you wore it to remind yourself—
a woman dressed in black.

I, too, was much the same,
at forty-five pot-bellied,
throwing the dirt in my face,
dirt from the grave,
the undertaker's hand on my shoulder.
I dreamed of the breasts
and thighs of young girls;
I stood before the mirror
as at a wake,
long hair, loud shirt and loud slacks;
at least I would go in style.

Then we got our new bodies.
Your hand touched my arm
and my face, a death mask, was clean;
all the dirt fell away, a truckload.
And the young girls died instead.

Your hand touched my arm
and you stood there in a white dress
like a woman after a bath. And you were beautiful.

Sheet-monger, blanket-hoarder,
small-breasted Annie, my skinny, my love,
the night we got our new bodies
we threw all the covers off.

Quicksilver Thing

Small-boned
quicksilver thing

you are
rising full-length

naked
in your looking

glass   Are
you offering

me strange
breasts swaying or

floating
somewhere on pink

toe shoes
turning those thighs

to the
world   Have I seen

passing
your reflection

that deep
secret room you

live in
alone   Mirror

girl my
shiny daughter

over
dreamy shoulders

have you
caught me today

watching
you drift away

An Interview with a Tornado Victim on April 16 1974
Never Shown on the CBS Evening News

Not that I would attribute
some force in nature
to her. But she did drop by
like a black funnel,
sweeping a path
across my life. Oh, there were
warnings, not the usual ones,
the siren on top of
the post office sounding three
times, the weather reports
on the radio.
But there were warnings all right,

not the air suddenly still,
muggy and strangling,
not the birds quiet as if
waiting, not the rain
and the dark sky.
Anyone who's ever lived
in the tornado belt knows them.
And there have been others
like me. You have to admit
a certain attraction,
looking back on it—
town, neighborhoods demolished.

And it will happen again.
Let's face it: I made
a mistake, am fortunate
to be standing here,
running out that
way, out the door, arms flung wide
like a man shouting "Here I am!"
the way you'd say of them:
"They're not right for each other;

she's too moody and he's
looking for trouble."
That was my first mistake, that

and leaving my family back
there in the house, left
calling me. I was lucky,
not really hit like
those in Xenia,
Ohio. Still there's picking
up to do, all the rebuilding.
My friends escaped and
are helping. Since in our town
I was the only one,
Nixon won't fly here
or talk about Hank Aaron.

Trying to Shovel Out

for R. B. L.

It's a daily
job, shoveling. Falling hard
it is building up
like guilt, my winter mother,
the heavy snow swirling down
around my house. All
that it can reach, touch,
turns cold in its freeze, my Ford
buried in the drive,
impotent like the children's
snowmen, the ice of its voice
that wind off the lake

shouting, telling
me what to wear: "Button up."
Quite a chill factor.
And I remember crying
forgiveness, my mother's arms:
"I will keep you warm;
you must be cold."
And though I love the snow, how
it wants to cover
our tracks—it is piled so high
you forget what's underneath,
a lost mitten, in

January
the Xmas tree that must wait
till April comes and
the thaw—when it settles down
(the way she settled into
her chair, head of our
family), I push
it back like a snowthrower,
like an angry scoop

to shovel out the driveway,
to clear a path for myself
as if to say *It's*

me here; I have
the right! It's a matter of
survival. What an
accumulation. You'd think
the old street light out in front
would soon feel threatened
the way that bank
inches up day after day
from the ground. Stupid,
I say: this is only snow
she's buried under back in
Dayton, Ohio.

**Turning Forty-five, after Drinks and Dirty Jokes
and Talk of Women, I Fall Asleep by the Fire and
Have a Vision**

The hush of this place,
night's snowfall,
tracks, ruts gone now.

The wind stops, a signal.
I know you are here
waiting for me, a young girl
I'd lie down into.

O my snow angel,
I would walk toward you,
snowshoeing, awkward at first,
into the woods.

First steps again.

Tom McKeown,born in Evanston, Illinois, in 1937, lives on Lake Michigan near Pentwater. His poems have been published in a number of magazines including *The Nation, Sumac,* and *Chelsea.* He has published three books of poems: *The Luminous Revolver* (1974), *Driving to New Mexico* (1974), and *The House of Water* (1974).

Photo by R. F. McKeown

Hair

Everyone is losing
his hair.
Hair is falling
like rain,
like grass torn
from its roots.

A clock shuffles out
of a house and tries
to save the hour,
tries to gain time
for the dying hair.

Nothing works.
Hair has covered up
the grass.
It makes me
think of sleep.

What shall I do?
I am the village barber.
I must cut hair, I must!
There are so many to feed:
a wife, a son, and nine
bald daughters.

The Lady in the Water Collection Department

It is raining in her room, rain has all
her notes, all her bills. Rain is almost
free as it comes through the roof,
unmeasured, unpurified. Someday she will
control all the rain. Now it is enough
to collect for water, stored water,
treated water.

At night she dreams water into sheets
and walls, water inside her watch, her rings
dissolving in water. Her hair is always
straight, always wet as if she is forever
ascending from some invisible lake. Almost
awake, almost drowning.

If her lover comes, he is very late. Riding
on a train without dimensions,
he finally arrives and undresses. He has
a blue clarity: he shines in the half-light.
When finally she reaches up, he slips easily
through her fingers, leaving her as much
alone as ever, looking down at the flooding
streets, water crowding the staircase
beneath her window.

Nude Climbing a Flagpole

What a funny thing for her to do!
With so many men around, she
couldn't miss. But she misses

everything: herself & her ardent
admirers. I am one of them. So
are you.

She climbs above us into clean air
with only a pole against her.

What more will she do to punish us?

In the Winter of Tigers

In the winter of tigers,
after the zoo closes, the sun
smokes and thins out, seeds
leap from an apple's core,
wheat whispers loudly
to the earth, to startled snow.

A crow plummets
through the calm sky
like a black parachute
that never opens.

In the middle of winter, the tigers
walk up the snowy mountains
and spread out with the snow,
until there is only snow and tigers,
and the memories of tigers,
invisible against the snow.

Floating the Ghost River

I float by woods and rocks
that have lived well
without human kindness.

At evening, I hear fire
straining its rude voice
as I curve toward sleep.

The hours pass bare and whole
into the sky,
pass under water,
unmarked, unused.

The river flows directions
I will never follow.

At times, the wilderness
is an altar: two elk
kneel down, antlers locked,
drooling
in a deathless calm.

The Desert World

petrified bones
embrace the wind

all directions
are lost to heat

here everyman is
blind to what
the sand
has accomplished

over and over
it has built
solitude
and destroyed it

all landmarks are
buried or splintered

each season runs
quietly into the next
there are no
celebrations

heat measures heat
rain the lovely lady
rarely shares
her favors

like the sea
the sand follows
its own tides
toward exhaustion

Inside the Vision of Peace

The world has gone inside itself
like a snake returning to its discarded skin.
A new wind blows over the fields
searching for the last salt sea.

The rain has gone through me with its glassy claws.
It has brought me back to the last day
when I sat in a tree made of stone
and watched the slow mastodons lifting their tusks
into the descending snow.

It was yesterday, it will be tomorrow; fish climbing
trees in the loud air, great armored birds wheeling
awkwardly in the cloudless sky. A sharp thorn carries
me into the present: blood under my thumbnail,
blood hardening in a white rose.

We turn in our beds like rusted keys that cannot
open doors. We examine the maps in our palms that lead
only to ourselves. The cold telephone rests
on the floor like a useless prayerstone.

Outside the mastodons are moving again. Great sheets
of ice are creaking, sliding toward me in the warm night.

Judith Minty (b. 1937), a native of Detroit, now lives in North Muskegon where she sails regularly on Lake Michigan. Her work has appeared in many literary magazines including *Poetry, The Seneca Review,* and *Southern Poetry Review.* Her first book is *Lake Songs and Other Fears,* and she has recently completed a second manuscript.

Palmistry for Blind Mariners

I. Preparations

Prepare for gypsies. Carry
plenty of silver. Layer yourselves
in warm clothes. The weather
is moody, sometimes flashes
dark eyes, then blues into Nordic ice.
Don't be afraid. I am
the captain, have sailed here before.

II. Casting Off

This hand is an island
surrounded by oceans. Cast off
from its heel. Forget the thumb. It lies
in other lakes that run deeper and I have
not yet charted the course there,
for they deal in births and deaths and we
are still young. Believe me,
this western coastline is safer. I know
there is joy in the journey,
but it is a long sail
of sleepless nights and you may go
days without sun. Hug close
to the shore. Sight
from stars. The lines
of rivers are visible, but seldom
open themselves to our lake. You will find
no port until Heartline.

III. Following the Dunes

Mount of the Moon is well traveled,
yet waves have chewed at its dunes,
cratered, devoured its face. We have no appetite
for steps that cascade to the lake
from a desert of shifting sand. Green
gropes for roots back in the cup of the palm.

This first part takes years,
but suffer the calm. Pass your childhood
in tepid waters. Learn poems, strum music, sleep,
study. Your reflection
lies in clear pools and drifting is easy.
These hills beam no dangerous stars.

Headline ahead, off the bow.
See wind fill the sail, but don't try
to enter that channel, for we draw too much water.
Take the tiller. Concentrate. Do not
run aground. Miles of shoreline
lie north yet to navigate.

Water is enemy to land. The sea builds.
It licks and curls round the point
and the dunes strike back. Beware
of logs. Flotsam floats in the swell
and tree stumps are spears at our hull.
Shield yourself. Stay aloof from the battle.

Squall lines stretch dark
over the horizon. Waves rise, angry. The wind
shifts. Come about, set your course, we must race
for the harbor. Mount of Mars gives courage
and sun glints inland on a plain
where Health and Life cross the path of Heart.

This lake has moods. Now gale warnings up.
The sea bares its teeth and wolves howl. Hurry.
Only two knots to Heartline
in that hollow of hills. Hear horns
at the pier, see the lighthouse. Let the wind
blow and the mast bend. Safety ahead.

IV. Heartline

This channel is long, goes fathoms
deep, a river that runs

through Muskegon, Grand Rapids, Lansing,
forks off toward Detroit.
But those narrows are death and we cannot
cruise them for, oh sailors,
there are so many here to love. Stay.
Drop anchor. Drift back with the current
from sunlight to moonrays.

Let the stream wash
over years as it laps against wrists.
Feel the chill of empty rooms change
as hands burn your body and blankets
cocoon around skin
that beads with a fear of new knowledge.
Cry out the old pain,
the breaking and separating, move on
as whispers lap against banks.

Touch willow branches without fingertips.
Swim after trout. Listen
for laughter. It is there in the night
fires, the call of cats, in the eagle's wing
as he soars toward the sun.
Weave water lilies into garlands and give them
as gifts. Gather stones for your house.
Live here always, if you can. This harbor
is haven for memories.

V. The North Woods

Summer passes too quickly. Winter
brings pain. The past
dries like straw flowers.
We must change camp before withering
begins. In this Indian Summer
the sun lowers its heavy flame
over the lake and glints
on arrows of my Chippewa brothers.

Our canoe is ready, stripped bark
from birch trees. We will travel
light, eat berries and roots
along the way, make footprints in sand.
Deer will drink from our hands and the hoot
of owls will guide us. We need no charts.
But I warn you, there will be
wailing and a beating of breasts.

Dip your paddle as you pass the bear
who sleeps at the foot of her dune
and mourns cubs, lost
in the crossing from Wisconsin.
Forget love-rites and matings
and children. Bury them
deep under Mercury's mound.
This lake and mothers are cruel.

Glide through vapors of fog.
Let them swirl around you, cling
like webs to your face and hair.
Hide in the mist. Creep
up the little finger. No clearing today,
only blindness. Grope
for land if you wish. Go ashore
if you are tired of seafaring.

For my part, I know this hand
and cannot turn in again.
If you must, follow me. I am going
past the islands out
into the lake. There is a place
I have heard of where you can sink
deep into the center of dreams, where waves
will rock you in sleep, where everything
is as you wished it to be.

Harbors

Evening and sailboats
anchored in the cove turn
slowly back and forth with the wind as if
they hear music. They bow
to shore and the sun
which, torn by gray clouds,
sinks into the wild island.

In August we turn
homeward to a harbor
where forests of masts stand planted
in wells. The boats
bob and clank their tambouring halyards as if
wanting to dance again. Their spars
cut the full moon.

Back on that island perhaps
the forest still whirls in the swamp.
When winds play
and the moon rounds,
and if an echo remains, gray masts
will step out from shore, leap
and spin over the empty bay.

The Fourth of July Drowning

They came for you, fumbling through fog,
the half-men, hunchbacked in black suits.
They searched for the echo of your cry,
for your shadow, for your hair floating up
like blind spider legs reaching for light.
Sunless they groped, fins pushing deeper.

Now under siren, through fog
and waves, they bring you to port
hunched, knees drawn up to your chin,
the black bag warm like new beginnings.
Tall women wait cold in the crowd
and remember their arms full of babies.

Prowling the Ridge

You, husband, lying next to
me in bed, growl
like a wild dog or wolf
as you travel the woods
of your dream.
I feel your legs running
from or after some

thing in the dark. Now you
turn and curl toward the moon.
Away from me, you
prowl along ridges and hunt
with the pack. You rest
your paws on their wild fur, bare
teeth to raw meat.

If I reach out and touch
the curve of your haunch,
brush my hand over your skin,
I can tame you
back to this room, to this wife
still outside
your blanket of sleep.

But it is your dream
I burn for, the other
place and time.
Wolf, leave tracks now. Quick.
Let me follow your scent.

Cynthia Nibbelink was born in 1947 on a farm in Iowa and now lives in Grand Rapids, where she teaches writing at Grand Valley State College. Her work has appeared in many magazines including *The Harvard Advocate, Once Again,* and *The Massachusetts Review.* A collection of poems, *Animals,* was published in 1972.

Photo by Ellen Nibbelink

Gypsies

i

And there were gypsies. Mother told me that. But not many of us
remember that far back. But I would ask her, *Mother, tell me about
the olden days.* And she did not flinch when I said *olden days,* she
never thought about being forty-four years old, or fifty-four, or
even sixty. And if you would look at her you would know: her
face has been content to grow old, there were so many things to
think about. But yes, gypsies, they came to get grain, they stole
small children, their men were handsome as night, or their men
were handsome and not to be trusted! *Remember that about men,
the handsome ones, remember that honey.* And at the country
school, after lunch one day all the children were out playing and
a caravan came by, and later they noticed, the teacher with her
stiff dark dress and her stiff dark voice asked, *And where, my
dears, is Alfred,* and no one but Jonathan could answer, but
Jonathan was holding his crotch like he couldn't wait much
longer so the stiff dark voice reprimanded him. To the bathroom!
And no one knew then that Jonathan could have answered,
because the gypsies had given Jonathan a beautiful dark red
stone to match his blood they said if ever he told. And they
scratched his wrist, and they made him write *Jonathan* on one
wheel. So Jonathan's name was inscribed in blood on one wagon
wheel of the gypsy caravan.

ii

So it wasn't till evening that the community, seven miles this
way, ten miles that way, the men got together, and the wives and
children got together in one house, and what should they do.
And the men brought ropes and guns. But each child told a
bigger story, how many of them there were, the caravan oh it
lasted forever! So the men put down their guns, because a gypsy
knows he knows the man who shoots, he can spot the gunman
who kills among twenty-five gunmen quick as lightning he
knows! And the gypsies don't forget. Next time they come back
it will be Jonathan.

iii

So bargain with them then. Give them a little wheat, some oats, the glass jars Peter and Treva brought across, and the old silver. And don't confront them, don't demand, go cautiously, cautiously. Why Alfred is too small anyway, surely they wanted Christopher, it was all a mistake. Till Alfred's mother is crying, *No no he's a strong boy, he's little but he works like a man my Alfy he's a man I tell ya he's a man, shoulda seen him with them shucks working right along-side his grandpa, Alfy Alfy Alfy!*

iv

The gypsies took things like it belonged to them. Mother was just young and married and alone in the house and the gypsies walked right on in, or they would have, but she bolted the front door and ran out using the back screen door, ran out to the men in the fields. And my father and Clarence told her it was alright. She could stay there. So Clarence came back, and said hello to the dark, handsome gypsy man who was just walking off with a pailfull of wheat and a shovel, and small tools from the shed. *Hello,* Clarence said, *Nice day, can I help you.* And the gypsy said, *No thank you, I think we have all we need, thank you.*

v

And I tell my husband now, I say, *Oh and there were gypsies, I even saw a whole long caravan one time and Mother and I were all alone and we locked the doors!*

I tell my husband, *There were gypsies!* But he does not believe me. He laughs. I say *Oh but they took things, you'd invite them in and when they left you'd notice the silver tray was missing, or the ornament Geertje sent from Germany. And they stole little children at the country schools!*

But my husband laughs. I say, *There were gypsies, and they took things like it belonged to them!*

But my husband does not believe me.

You're crazy, he says. *Crazy woman, crazy woman, you're a gypsy. How'd I ever end up marrying such a crazy woman.* And, *I'd do it again,* he says, *yeah, I'd do it again.*

My husband is dark and handsome and not to be trusted.

He laughs.
He does not believe me.

Cynthia Nibbelink

How Can I Say It Any Other Way

The sun is more fire than blood today!
And I am leaping
into the hot white walls
of the sun's mouth
My own teeth are more gold than ivory!
My lips more fruit than red!
My heart a gay old celebration!
And my eyes, my eyes are each end of a rainbow
their many colors all one sea

so deep

My whole body
open
like the fan of a peacock glistening
just after rain!

I fly to the top of your sails, and we
represent every nation!

Look now, my love
look now

You will never see
such incredible horizons again!

Black Lake

My husband calls them "The Nomads."
The whole treeless camp at Ottawa Beach
on a misty evening, skinny kids running
everywhere, green tents and pick-up trucks,
old cars parked just where they stopped.
And mothers huddling under ratty umbrellas
with a hand-knit poncho wrapped around the baby.
Here and there the glow of a charcoal fire.
Puffs of smoke rising from hamburg and hotdog suppers.

But I think of Steinbeck, and of
the lady I lived with for six weeks once in Utah.
She was an Okie herself, she told me,
and didn't know where her family was now,
but the girls all had names like flowers:
hers was "Fern."

And I notice how tired the mothers seem,
husbands out fishing or sleeping.
And I think of this rainy, monotonous day, the
way kids do finally run out of games inside
a tent, and I hear the whine of children,
small scratched feet wander toward a familiar umbrella at last.
Soiled bandaids float in the water.

I smell the crisp black edge of a sizzling hotdog.

And a nursing mother looks over to her neighbor's
umbrella, nods and smiles at how hard the other's child sucks.
She waves, blows a fly off her own sleeping baby's eye-lid.

Nomads for a week, or a weekend.

"There's something good about it," I say to my husband.
"You can tell. These people are friends."

And I wonder if they have an agreement
to name all their girls for flowers, or
if their sons all have an uncle in the family somewhere
who was a sea-captain,
or caught the biggest fish.

Out of the Gaping Distance

Just before I sleep
I see the blue flowers again
again the long white stems
young girls blowing home across the fields

in this land where no man hears no man
where at night you face yourself a stranger
in the shadows you have already disappeared from
suddenly
out of the gaping distance
a twisted cry
moon split open
the old wolf barks

just before I sleep
not daring to open my eyes
to see nothing

and in the morning they will say
oh pooh-hooh it was a dead cry
it was a dead wolf
no moon
no moon
no moon

The Motive for Metaphor

I want to be *beautiful*, Mama,
she said, hoisting up her big grapefruit
breasts the blue sweater could not control,
I want to be like the other kids, Mama,
she said, Oh I have got such a crooked nose
and my teeth are all ugly, and my feet,
even John's buckle boots don't fit
Oh Mama if you knew how all the kids tease—
how did I grow up this *big*, Mama,
how come I got to be such a big lunker, Mama, Mama, look—
I ain't gonna go! I ain't gonna go! I ain't gonna go!

Howard Norman, born in Toledo, Ohio, in 1949, has traveled throughout Canada and the Caribbean working on translation projects. His work has appeared in *Poetry Northwest, Panjandrum, Hawaii Review, The Iowa Review,* and many other magazines. *The Wishing Bone Cycle,* a collection of Cree translations, will be published soon.

Who-Tapped-the-Frogs-In

"First thing to know is
he was blind
so he walked along the stream
a different way.

He had a long stick and made his way
with it.

Frogs sat along the bank
listening and singing at the same time
UNTIL they heard that stick coming near
on the ground. Then each frog
jumped in!

And that's how this boy knew
where the water was—by the sound
those frogs made jumping in.
Now you know.

He followed the stream
out and back.

Keeping his feet dry that way.

All along the edge."

from the Cree of Samuel Makidemewabe

Dried Things Out

One job she had was to dry fish
with smoke or in the sun, and did this
well. Some of her name came from that.

Some days you could see her
stand in the water and find things
to dry there, too, grasshoppers
or dragonflies the wind sent into the
lake.

Or they flew into the water themselves
because they saw clouds
and high branches
reflected on the water
and thought they were flying UP
into the sky!

She would pick them up and hold them
in her hand, or put them
on a rock in the sun.
To dry their wings.

She would dry her wet skin
too, sometimes with a dragonfly
on each knee.

All three drying in the sun.

Some of her name
came from that.

from the Cree of Samuel Makidemewabe

Born Tying Knots

When he came out, into the world,
the umbilical cord was around his toes.
This didn't trouble us,
that he was tying knots THAT EARLY.
We untied it.

Later, he heard his birth
story.
It caused him to begin tying knots *again*.
He tied things up near his home,
TIGHT, as if everything might float away
in a river.

This river came from
a dream he had.

House things were tied up
at night. Shirts, other clothes too,
and a kettle. All those things
were tied to his feet so they would not
float away in the river he dreamed.
You could walk in
and see this.

Maybe the dream stopped.
because it was no longer comfortable
to sleep with shirts tied to him.
Or a kettle.

After the dream no longer came,
he stopped tying things,
EXCEPT for the one night he tied up
a small fire.
Tied up a small-stick fire!
The fire got loose its own way.

from the Cree of Samuel Makidemewabe

Many Voices

We were out gathering full ripe
berries.
The black ones with spitting seeds
in them. We were gathering those berries.
That's when she made a voice.
Her first one of the day!
It was not her own human voice, BUT IT CAME OUT
of her. It was fox barking noise she made.
I listened hard to make sure.

I heard a fox bark
in that voice. Maybe she was *thinking*
of a fox barking, long ago,
and that thinking CAME OUT LOUD.
If that's the way it worked.
I sat in shade
to listen.

Then there was just the sound
of her picking berries again.
Until her basket filled up.
And belly, too.

On the way home I heard CRICKET
noises. I heard a cricket
and turned over some stones
to find it. And a wet stump.
I couldn't find one.

Then I looked
at her. I should have known!
She got quiet
as if I'd lifted a stone off HER.
When I looked straight at her
she got quiet, yes, because that's how it goes
with a cricket
when its stone is lifted.

from the Cree of Samuel Makidemewabe

Rain Straight Down

For a long time we thought this boy
loved ONLY things that fell straight
down. He didn't seem to care
about anything else.

We were afraid he could only HEAR
things that fell straight down!

We watched him stand outside
in rain. Later, it was said
he put a tiny pond of rain water
in his wife's ear
while she slept. And leaned over
to listen to it.

I remember he was happiest talking
about all the kinds of rain.

The kind that comes off heron's wings
when they fly up from a lake. I know
he wanted some of that heron rain
for his wife's ear too!

He walked out in spring to watch
the young girls rub wild onion under their eyes
until the tears came out.
He knew a name for that rain too.

Sad onion rain.

That rain fell straight down
too, off their faces,
and he saw it.

from the Cree of Samuel Makidemewabe

Sat in the Center

This boy went out in a snow blizzard
to catch fish. He went out on the swamp ice
and brought his ice chisel with him
to dig a hole through it.
He went singing.
In summer we could hear that swamp
sing all its birds and frogs together, BUT THIS WAS
IN WINTER.
He was the only one singing.

We heard him dig the ice hole
in the distance, but we could not see
this. It was a chewing sound
his work made. After a while we got worried
he fell in.
Or that the snow snakes curled him
away.

Worried we would never again
see him bob up among the wood duck
decoys, LAUGHING!
In summer.

He stayed out on the ice
until night. Then we saw his torch-stick fire
moving toward us,
and he came BACK HOME to put the fish he caught
on the fire.
Our worrying did not stop there.
He sat with us and watched the fish thaw
and cook.

He sat with us
in the center, shivering.
THEN we heard his laughing thaw out
too.
That's when our worrying stopped.

from the Cree of Samuel Makidemewabe

Linda Parker, born in Illinois in 1942, lives on a farm near Ypsilanti where she is currently a writer-editor for ADP Network Services, Cybernetics Division. She has published in several literary magazines including *Chelsea*, *The Ann Arbor Review*, and *Harpers*.

Photo by Don Fostle

Brush Mask

Dreaming of the ebony
boat he will launch
to cross the sound,
he watches his onions grow

As the evening nurse
packs ice to break
his fever, blue
flannel to cover his legs.

Dozing by an old radio
like an elephant moving
away from a water hole,
mud flecking his hide,

He asks them to find
the alphabets he
lost somewhere between
the silo and the barn.

The Country Alphabet

1

These are my people;
these are their faces
lit in a last moon
whole in itself.

Piled in the dust
the white lumber of
the new farm house
returns to its tree,
when the moon is half-red
and all the hens are asleep.

In my mother's light,
this milk glass lamp
shines on the field:
it is green once more.

There you sit as always
in your uncle's lap,
his red cigar smoke
blowing toward the barn.

The farm chairs are dark
as the Bible whose old
chapters are scattered across
the floor: Jesus hangs on the wall
calling us to touch
the storm with our bare hands.

2

My grandmother was strong
in the country that gave her
heart its air, kept her closets
sweet where she took a flowered

dress off a hanger each morning
and wore it to the garden.

And in the garden she told me
how the master touched her
a thousand years ago,
his sweet face
catching sun this
side of the cross.

He gave me his robe, she said,
this dark blue scrap of wool,
this woolen patch that
covers these frosted windows.

The master,
my stained glass window
that breaks into roses,
the master
who stumbled like a sheep
that could not find the gate.

Take my hand, she said
to me, I will walk with you
to the bush that
bursts into flowers and
gives you a branch so
new ones will form.

But you will always carry
the death of the cow in the barn,
her blood, dark as a violet,
her hips, torn at the shanks.

You will carry
her death to the tree
and lay it down.

3

She went mad early and
began to shake the moon
off the blankets and quilts;
she forgot to be generous,
to feed the poor cats
starving in the barn.

She said she would need
turpentine to wash this year—
the clay was so bad,
so hard to get off the shirts.

Take the last door in the hall
she said, to the room where
my husband slept. This is
his white iron bed.

And its white iron
glows in that back room
where his sickness slid down
the posts and entered
even the garden.

4

In the cemetery, they have
toppled the holy stones and
taken the seed.

My grandmother will be buried there
beside him at a rural intersection.
A gas station will pump fuel
near the cemetary gates and
someone else's flowered dresses
will hang in the closet
facing the barn.

The tin bird on the barn roof
kept its direction
until he went blind and
they covered his feet
in unending clover.

5

They are not coming
home tonight, the dead.
Out beyond the hogs they lie
in a strange pasture
behind a white church
stuffed with old hay
and broken windows.

The hickory that marked us all
marks these new shadows;
the hickory
drops fruit on both
sides of the fence and
we lie down in our
individual weaknesses and
spread our arms
as it did, then set
the jars in line for winter,
stuffed with its fruit.

The intrusions on
that tree are past, where
they bargained the cost
of these acres.

6

This is what we came for,
to touch the old potatoes
in the dark cellar,
to take these stairs.

This was the winter
my grandmother kept seeds in a jar.
This was the winter
the seeds turned black.

This is the last country song.
These are the twelve cows
caught in the barn we
harvest when the madness
comes back—when the bird,
throat half-torn, cannot
lift its wings across the roof
and the plow horse dies
blind in the pasture.

This is what we came for.
This is the fire that
breaks across the road
bringing sense to the west woods,
where the grass is white;
it was always white
in our pastures.

Advice to the Lovelorn

They are aging in attic
beds that have no pelts
and drink from goblets
that are oxidizing:

there are ten thousand
beds in the dark
that are not beds,
where no animal bones
move in the sheets.

I have a house
that breaks into flowers
when my old animal
comes back to spread
himself across my skin.

He is a sheep fur
white and curled;
even in sleep his eyes
are my road lights
through night country.

Flood Disaster in Gallup, New Mexico

a storm moves
behind the old churches
and they hear rains
beginning to tear
their red ground

a squad car
sends blue flowers
into the sky as it
chases a young navajo
through the alleys
and bus depot

gallup gallup gallup
your ponies are loose
your squash blossoms
will be crushed

put your turquoise
rings in sandbags
and pitch them
against the trader's
windows and locks

get your pawn and
get your woman
the river is coming
get out of gallup
gallup gallup gallup

Dudley Randall was born in Washington, D.C., in 1914. He is
founder and editor-in-chief of Detroit's Broadside Press and a
librarian at the University of Detroit. He is the editor of several
anthologies of Black poetry including *More to Remember* (1970)
and *The Black Poets* (1971), and the author of many books,
including *After the Killing* (1973), and recently, co-editor of *A
Capsule Course in Black Poetry Writing* (1975).

Photo by Kwadwo Oluwale Akpan

Dudley Randall

Frederick Douglass
and the Slave Breaker

I could have let him lash me
like a horse or a dog
to break my spirit.
Others never lifted a finger.
I would have been just one more.

But something in me said, "Fight.
If it's time to die, then die for something.
And take him with you."

So all day long we battled,
the man and the boy, sweating,
bruising, bleeding . . .

till at last the slave breaker said,
"Go home, boy. I done whupped you enough.
Reckon you done learned your lesson."

But I knew who it was that was whipped.
And the lesson I learned
I'll never forget.

Booker T. and W. E. B.
(Booker T. Washington and W. E. B. Du Bois)

"It seems to me," said Booker T.,
"It shows a mighty lot of cheek
To study chemistry and Greek
When Mister Charlie needs a hand
To hoe the cotton on his land,
And when Miss Ann looks for a cook,
Why stick your nose inside a book?"

"I don't agree," said W. E. B.,
"If I should have the drive to seek
Knowledge of chemistry or Greek,
I'll do it. Charles and Miss can look
Another place for hand or cook.
Some men rejoice in skill of hand,
And some in cultivating land,
But there are others who maintain
The right to cultivate the brain."

"It seems to me," said Booker T.,
"That all you folks have missed the boat
Who shout about the right to vote,
And spend vain days and sleepless nights
In uproar over civil rights.
Just keep your mouths shut, do not grouse,
But work, and save, and buy a house."

"I don't agree," said W. E. B.,
"For what can property avail
If dignity and justice fail?
Unless you help to make the laws,
They'll steal your house with trumped-up clause.
A rope's as tight, a fire as hot,
No matter how much cash you've got.
Speak soft, and try your little plan,
But as for me, I'll be a man."

"It seems to me," said Booker T.–

"I don't agree,"
Said W. E. B.

Spring Before a War

Spring came early that year.
Early the snow melted and crocuses took over
And in dooryard gardens blossomed the flower of the
  slain Greek boy.
Before the spring retired came roses
And orange lilies and great blanched spheres of peonies.
Days were warm and bright and fields promised incredible
  harvests,
And in meadows fresh and unscarred
With waists encircled and flanks touching
Strolled the dead boys
And the widowed girls.

Abu

Abu
's a stone black revolutionary.
Decided to blow up City Hall.
Put full-page ad
in *New York Times*
announcing his inten/
                    shun.
Says rightinfrontof
F.B.I. in fil/
            trators
he gon sassinate
rich white liberal
gave only *half*
a million
to N.A.A.C.P.
Says nothing 'bout that Southern sheriff
killed three black prisoners
'cept, he admire him
for his sin/
            cerity.

Tell It Like It Is

Tell it like it is.
Lies won't get it.
Foaming at the mouth won't get it.
Defamation of character won't get it.

If you want to be virile,
be virile,
but you ain't gonna get virile
by saying somebody else ain't virile,
And if the white boys are all faggots,
like you say,
how come we got all these black poets
with yellow skin?

George

When I was a boy desiring the title of man
And toiling to earn it
In the inferno of the foundry knockout,
I watched and admired you working by my side,
As, goggled, with mask on your mouth and shoulders
    bright with sweat,
You mastered the monstrous, lumpish cylinder blocks,
And when they clotted the line and plunged to the floor
With force enough to tear your foot in two,
You calmly stepped aside,

One day when the line broke down and the blocks
    clogged up,
Groaning, grinding, and mounted like an ocean wave
And then rushed thundering down like an avalanche,
And we frantically dodged, then placed our heads
    together
To form an arch to life and stack them,
You gave me your highest accolade:
You said, "You not afraid of sweat. You strong as
    a mule."

Now, here, in the hospital,
In a ward where old men wait to die,
You sit, and watch time go by.
You cannot read the books I bring, not even
Those that are only picture books,
As you sit among the senile wrecks,
The psycopaths, the incontinent.

One day when you fell from your chair and stared at
    the air
With the look of fright which sight of death inspires,
I lifted you like a cylinder block, and said,
"Don't be afraid
Of a little fall, for you'll be here
A long time yet, because you're strong as a mule."

Green Apples

What can you do with a woman under thirty?
It's true she has a certain freshness, like a green apple,
but how raw, unformed, without the mellowness of maturity.

What can you talk about with a young woman?
That is, if she gives you chance to talk,
as she talks and talks and talks about herself.
Her self is the most important object in the universe.
She lacks the experience of intimate, sensitive silences.

Why don't young women learn how to make love?
They attack with the subtlety of a bull,
and moan and sigh with the ardor of a puppy.
Panting, they pursue their own pleasure,
forgetting to please their partner, as an older woman does.

It's only just that young women get what they deserve.
A young man.

Danny L. Rendleman, born in Flint in 1945, is living again in Flint where he teaches in the Writing Lab at the University of Michigan–Flint. His poems have appeared in many magazines including *Epoch, Field, Sumac,* and *Granite,* and he has published two books of poems: *Signals to the Blind* (1972), and *Winter Rooms* (1975).

Photo by Stan Blood

Midland

In the grim
furrows of his knuckles
and the sharp
new moons of his nails
my father planted
acacia and wintergreen
plum and asphodel
iris and jackpine.

Nothing grew, all to seed
or wrist-thick weeds
and clutter.
So he learned the round
beauty of the common,
carving hairy roots
to the likeness of his children,
peeling the skin from his wife
to find how well she thrived
in a wet, short spring.

These labors too withered
and fed a neighbor's plot.
Now he tills the open field,
reaching to pull the stars
out and down like ribbons,
singing coarsely to himself,
promising stones in the next county
to rebuild the fence,
to dance more slowly,
to do without.

Letter from Olga, Declaiming

The whores of Naples
have trees for thighs,
old family willows,
chuckling over reunions,

loud in the face with birds,
the colorful, wild-eyed kind
that paint the seascapes
with narrow palettes, palette knives.

The whores of Naples
are made of rope, the Ace
Hardware kind, an inch-thick
sort for country hangings,

spittum on their propane lips
that hisses up a hell of their own,
wetness to play stride piano,
kisses to bless the vinegar.

The whores of Naples
have large thumbs, green eyes
to fondle themselves and
round boiling-red babies.

Where they live sweet-pea
clambers over the rotted fence
and the elders stagger to the stream
to piss away the afternoon by the hour.

The Parting Chores

The roses, too, need pruning,
to be cut knee-high, pulled

from where they clutch the house,
snagged in the siding. There is

an odd light roosting in the leaves,
out of breath, Oriental-eyed.

Your poems make room on my desk,
baroque as pears, like my new home,

the yellow trim peeling, warm as
eyebrows. My hands smell of ash,

the end of winter fires, summer storms.
Your poems are brown and Jewish

seed on my sill that urge themselves
open like hands from around handles.

Just now I went in to move the toys
from my blond boy's face as he slept,

restless, dreaming, trying to remember
my name. He cannot remember you at all,

couldn't if he did not hear his father
nightly reciting sketches toward a painting

of you heavy with him, setting the clock,
staring down the dawn in disbelief.

Yet another season seeps in sly as wine,
a list of duties long as your arm:

cutting, painting, forgetting the past.
Everything aimed to retain the virginal,

that bright silent spot in us that will
not bruise, but offers up scars like new moons.

Tenant

Unsucked dugs asway
Aunt Edna readies for bed

Her dress-shields off
Fat and floral-gowned wide

False teeth pink & bubbling
In a bedside glass of stale water

She grunts trimming
Her corns and nails with a razor blade

Pin-curled diabetic
Widowed twice

She's invented life
So many times

Nothing's the same day to day
Except routine

The growing old
Toward a misspelled obituary

And the faint music of swan
Decals peeling in the john

Where the seat is never lifted
By any man

Rosalie

Dull as an eraser the moon
bends down and promises anything
but her namesake.

We called her Rosie. Her gleam
could water plants while
you were away.

Her crossed brown legs could
undo any hex, could set you straight
for a dime.

Where are the cemeteries
in a city? And who has the sharpened
spade for the grave?

She wasn't quite right coming
into this round world,
and was not lovely going out.

The Drowned Darling

Didn't the water rinse off
your hour-old smell of sex?

It flowed away silver into
the thick bright reeds?

Wasn't it noon: and
your black hair slick

down narrow shoulders where
gills had no time to form?

The green current pulled
your many silences downstream

and the doors of your skin
finally opened to the knock

of the sun grinning
like a bald salesman.

The Death of Neruda

Walking to your house
down a road
not yet paved over

the woods on either side
like damp rumpled clothes
chill but not yet winter

Your dog meets me half-way
so you must be home
saving me some whiskey

some smoke and some story
of still another siren
languishing in your absence

A deer starts from the trees
quivers in my path
and bounds on across and gone

and knowing he shouldn't the dog
looks at me guiltily
and dives after the white-tail

I pause and listen until the barking
trails off far away
and hear the wetness click

I turn back towards home
watching the yellow west
go gray and sequined

thinking I'll read the evening news
to see what's happening
who's dead or not and who's dying

Lawrence Russ, born in Detroit in 1945 and currently living in Ann Arbor, has published poems in several magazines including *The Nation, The Iowa Review, New York Quarterly,* and *Chelsea.*

Photo by Pauline Lubens

The House-Trailer

One night, crossing a muddy field,
I found a house-trailer propped up on blocks.
Through the window I could see
papers spread on a battered cardtable.
On the wall, a beige raincoat hung
by the loop at the neck.
The coat, the whole trailer
was a body deserted by its soul:
a comfort, like a friend
who accepts his own failures.

Not Speaking

A young wife stands at the kitchen
sink, immobile in the roar
of the garbage disposal, eyes
fixed on the small black hole.
Her hands rest on the counter's edge.
Droplets have covered her fingers and knuckles
and the fine spray continues
like gravel that flies up
when a car starts to skid off the road.

Holy, Holy, Holy

You lie asleep on your back.
Your breasts
are incredible mosques
content not to rise toward any heaven,
warm in the cool night of Istanbul.

But inside them
hundreds of pious celibates
run around crazed,
huddling in clusters,
flinching away from the molten walls,
blinded by red light
that steams from floor and ceiling!

They cry out, they weep
for their lost
childhoods, when they were happy
with their twigs
and magnifying glasses,
torturing ants.

from **Grandfather**

Old stick of bitterness, you wanted
to beat us all from your door,
even if you had to die to do it.
So Grandpa, only those insects,
your brothers,

scraped out music for your death.
I remember the skull caps,
the stained white of prayer-shawls,
and your face like a fist
unclenched at last.

The Weights

In California you feel as if daylight
will last forever,
but even there
red vines crawl over the door,
the tree's shadow lengthens on the lawn
like an arm reaching for the house.

I don't want to end
in the crystal paperweight,
locked in the doll-house.

I don't want to die like a hand in a pocket.

I am the boy
who wanted to fly, not caring how,
vampire or comic-book hero,
and I ask that boy's forgiveness
and all the things I hid from,
for the weights I carry.

The Turning

And what if the little girl playing with her doll
suddenly feels it
watching her, the eyes alive
like the eyes of the fish
mother sliced open on the kitchen counter?

Does she continue her play in that dark basement,
that stillness like a bicycle wheel
spinning in air
after the rider has fallen off?

Or does she turn away
to the daylight of hungry dogs
and other children?

The Child

He had to learn the way a staircase
climbs without moving.
He knew the trees
talked together; not knowing particular
signs, but understanding
their hard, isolate trunks,
their branches shaking before a rain.

And then one night to walk out
beyond the people's voices,
the hide-and-seek and statues,
beyond the brick houses
into the field
where two cats chase moths
through weeds and bushes, mingling with the black
scraping of crickets.

He sat in the prickle of night grass,
the half-moon behind him,
and took out his book of matches.
He burned his hand in the field, to seal
his marriage to the several fires
that cannot be touched for long.

Lives

for Mary

The trucker feels how calloused
his hands have grown
from miles of pavement shaking the wheel.
He blows the diesel's horn, and becomes
the night ghost of two small towns,
of billboards and roadside ditches.
The trucker is not on good terms
with the moon.
It reminds him of a car with one headlight out,
and as it comes at you
you can't tell which one.
The moon stays above the hood, unmoving
like a silver dollar lost
to a slot machine ten years ago,
or a round-faced wife who sits up all night
staring at the door.

———

The boy is deaf. His mother sees him off, explains
to the stewardess, who boards him first.
When the husband and wife come on
they find him in the seat next to theirs. He cries
quietly, waving at the terminal, nervously
sliding the window-cover up
and down. Slowly, the husband begins to feel
as if he is the one
who sees his parents behind glass,
the one making
sounds in his throat.
As the plane taxis out on the runway
he stares past the boy, at the pavement, the brown
stubble, the overcast sky.

———

The woman in the ticket booth, shut
behind glass, speaking through metal slits,
is sick of the lines of people:
the ugly ones, the slick ones, all
the fumbling hands.
As she tucks in her blouse where it's loosened
her arm brushes her breast,
and she feels the small heat.
But she's never believed she's pretty,
and she's done with the dank smells that pass for love.
She's come to expect disappointment.
Last year she saw a man shoot himself
in front of the theater;
that night, she dreamed he understood
her sadness, and that he made love to her.
Now she doesn't care if no one comes
to the late night showing.

———

High above the ground, his room is dark,
pens like broken twigs on the desk.
The man is tired.
His black umbrella, rolled up tight,
tilts in the corner—
so thin, so much without dreams.
He's tired of boiling water,
of looking through the wrong end of darkness
at the streets so shriveled and far.
He thinks of a woman in another city,
her hazel eyes, and long hair;
he wants to hold her, to talk with her.
He wants a poem like a honeycomb
of sadness and fire, sweating with gold.
On the road far below, cars drive
through the dark, their beams turned down,
like desires searching for a chest to enter.

Herbert Scott (b. 1931), a native of Oklahoma, worked in the grocery business for eleven years in Illinois, Oklahoma, and California, before moving to Michigan in 1968. He is now associate professor of English at Western Michigan University. His first book of poems, *Disguises,* was published in 1974 and a second book, *Groceries,* is forthcoming.

The Fear of Groceries

A man goes to a grocery store to buy
a can of peaches. Returning home
and opening the can for his supper
he discovers not peaches, but a heart.
He slumps to the floor of his kitchen
holding the heart in his lap like a fish.
The label, he checks again, reads *peaches,*
he is sure, or does it say *fishes?*
He looks at the fish in his lap,
his finger hooked in its mouth.
Very much like a heart, he says.
He bends his head to cry and sees
his children's faces reflected in the red eyes
of the heart, the glossy, salmon heart.
His children are spawning,
or drowning in an ocean, their faces
very like the halves of canned peaches.

Butcher's Dream

I seen a cat once,
its head pasted
to the pavement
by the wheel of a car,
but its legs don't know it,
the whole body scrambling
to get up, to get loose.
I always wished I could work
with live meat, the red salt
crusting on my wrist.
I should of been a doctor.
I used to worry
what is the tenderest part
of the human carcass.
Then I seen some cannibal said,
the palm of the hand.
A delicacy you can't find
in other game. He'd kill
for the human hand.
How do you figure?
Not even a meal.
But it makes you wonder.
It makes you look
at your own hand
like a strange animal.

Checker

Checker is beautiful,
dark, shiny, hair,
breasts gentle as mares'
noses, easy gaited.
She doesn't like it
when Pet Foods
grabs her breasts
in the back room.
She knees him in the groin.
"They think you're meat
and they're bone," she says.
But she doesn't mind Bag Boy
feeling her legs
behind the checkstand
when he reaches for the sacks.
She knows he's not serious,
just passing the time of day.

The Clerk's Dream

I'm going to save
my money and someday
buy a store in the neighborhood,
me and my wife will run it,
I'll be my own boss,
and when I take money
out of the till
it will be my money,
and I'll open when
I feel like it, and close
when I feel like it,
I'll wear a flannel shirt
and no tie, when my kids
get home from school
they'll stock the shelves,
they'll be cute as shit
in their little aprons,
and wait on customers,
I figure I'll make
maybe twenty grand a year
and I'll join the Junior Chamber
of Commerce, and maybe
the Lions, I'll let my wife off
one afternoon a week
to play cards with the Jaycee
Janes, and on Christmas
I'll pack a apple box
with bent cans and busted cereal
and maybe even a turkey
and take it to the church
to give to them less
fortunate.

Cracked Eggs

"Any cracked eggs today?"
The old woman lifts her face
to me like a cratered moon.
I shake my head. Later,

in the back room,
I find her sucking
cracked eggs, a bucket
of them at her feet,

plucking the shells
from between her teeth
like the stems of strawberries,
a beard of yellow on her chin.

Surprised, she stutters an excuse,
broken speech twisting
like bones in her throat,

then hurries to the door,
old mother, wrapping
the shambles of her dignity
in the flapping wings of her coat.

Boss's Dream

She come in one morning,
sassy as spring. I said,
Mam, you sure got long legs.
She smiled. I said, I bet
they come together
like the intersection
of Cedar and Vine. She said,
I bet you know the way
to get there from here.
We drove west of town,
back into Beecher's woods,
walked a quarter mile
through brush, wild grape
and onions, piled leaves under
a cottonwood shedding fur,
her legs branched out.
It was good in there.
Later, she had to take
a leak, squatted down
in the leaves and pissed
in her shoes. All the way
back to the car, her shoes
squishing, laughing to beat hell.
The best it ever was.
I'd of give her the keys to the store,
but she never come back.

The Lost Aisles

There are aisles
we have not discovered
where a man and woman
are making love.
We hear her calling
his name, his name
is a song falling
beneath our feet.

All who enter
the lost aisles
must walk barefoot,
must carry
what they own,
must own their voices
lifting in praise.

In the lost aisles
when the lovers
have finished
the man lies still
within the woman, waiting
for her to rouse.
She does not push
him away, but holds him

in her arms
and legs, holds him
like a tree, the fruit
still falling around them.
They may eat
without leaving
each other's bodies.

The lovers may be lost
in any aisle
we cannot discover,

they may be waiting
for us to come, gather
the fruit in our arms,
gather them in our arms.

Eve Shelnutt was born in South Carolina and is now living in
Kalamazoo where she teaches creative writing at Western
Michigan University. Her fiction and poetry have appeared in
*Shenandoah, The Virginia Quarterly Review, The Greensboro
Review,* and others. She is working now on a collection of poems
titled *Air and Salt.*

Family

The sun has left the middle of the sky,
the earth is turning swamp.
My father changes wives, my mother men
who live with us; we multiply.
At night we keep the lights off in the hall.
We dream in pairs:
who tends the dove, who sends it out?

Family Getting Back to God

The day the father dies,
the mother calls him James.
She has him burned, the ashes stored;
the children crack like gourds.
They try to shake him out;
him moving sound is sin.
The children's waists grow slim;
sand falls through.
Then they are laying silver
cross-boned by the plates,
hiding notes saying
GOD KNOWS beneath the sugar bowl.
Cynthia learns the parts of fish
by taking fish apart.
Anne is counting colors in the salt.
They bless the supper:
Let the supper work.
They lift the mother up.

Setting
for my father

Three hands rest
like goblets by the plates.
Three engraved with waiting
in our laps.
Yes, your daughters are learning
how to behave.
But the body is so rich
it will all come up.

Grandfather

Night, children,
is the blue mane of a horse
covering the sun.
Death is one hair more.
I will buy you a pinto and oats.
When night is darker than licorice,
rub his mane
softly as a candle lights a wall.
Ask for a ride.

Advantages

From watching gulls dive
in the impossible distance,
you know where fish travel in schools.
Long after the sun is gone,
the small of your back remembers
the burning of its other life. Soon
you will sleep on one crooked arm, the hand
an open shell from these depths.
In it is a gift I have made for you
which you will call *the moon*
until it rises and gives light.

Gift
for a mother

Is death her wedding dress?
Suddenly she is lovely, this sleep
peau de soie and fine seed pearl.
In another world, her daughters
hold a train of sorrow. Yet
this raised dome could be the slipper
perfect for the longest dance.
They can only imagine: hearts of elves,
lorn voices seeping through pine forest.
Halfway through a story which could go on
forever, keeping the children awake,
they settle on needles, close the muted light.
What woman *needs* a prince of only bones,
now the courting is over? Her daughters sleep;
they do not dream.

Visit

He drives up shadowed in insect wings
breaking on the windshield like lace.
Two brown spots mark the deaths of birds;
I come loose from the house.

For a week he drives me through light and dark,
under rice, through accidental fires.
He tells me I am not lost;
he sings me a hymn of Mary Magdelene.

He is used to this country of good roads.

The Widows

Seven days a week
we boil eggs for supper.
No more lying about loveliness.

At St. Mary's for the Aged

She thinks God wants a wife.
She would like to lie with Him.
Would He make her pretty,
or take her as she is?
Where, around Him, do the arms go?

The jealous Sisters see her rise;
their hands cross on the door.
She dies and, dead,
is not denied.
The Sisters lifting bones
are satisfied.

All-Hallows Children

Simon Peter is slaying the roosters;
the moon fills with blood, each
broken wing a mullion in the light.
But the disciples whisper they will have him
if it takes a winter of thorns.
They will have him dressed as himself,
in eyes.
So when the children flock out with baskets
and tongues of cockscomb,
they are told to ask for eggs.
Will the Pope look through a tracery of rose
when the windows crystallize?
The voice of one disciple adds:
If his eyes do not form the shape
of perfect future misery, next to which Judas
is nothing,
open the holes in your hands.

See, Rosicrucians, how the moon spills,
how thirty stars toss themselves
across a sudden cloth?

Separate

Here, the sky is colorless and fluid.
It is almost winter; birds
sharpen their eyes, their wings
stir color from the trees.
Time makes its own concoction, sweet
or leavened with thorns.
I will remember myself as a child
seated at my mother's table. Fork, knife
and spoon perfectly flank my plate.
She arrives with Portugese Easter bread
which hides an egg inside.
Always, then, I found it,
blessing the broken loaf.

Skaidrite Stelzer was born in Berchtesgaden, Germany, in 1947, and at the age of four she came to the United States. She now lives in Kalamazoo and attends Western Michigan University where some of her work has appeared in student publications.

Photo by Vija Doks

Progenitor

Grandmother laughs
from the potato field,
ignoring all the wrinkled little men
hiding beneath her skirts.
They will be her children;
their gnomish looks
do not disturb her.
"It is all a joke,"
she says, waving her blue cloak
like a faded eyelid.

You are watching her hair,
hoping she won't open her mouth any wider,
you are afraid she won't have any teeth.
But as it turns out they are all gold-capped,
reflecting so many small you's.
"It is a joke,"
grandmother laughs,
and keeps planting potatoes.

Fish-Dream

the night shakes loose
like the inside of an old shoe
the smells of sidewalks
sifting through the air.
things start rubbing apart
the small grains in furniture
unwrap themselves
start their usual dance.
the eyes and hands of lovers
wink from curtain folds,
occasionally
a salamander
winds across the ceiling
and small mirror-fish
flash behind my eyes.
I reach to touch something, but
night only deals in half-forms
the quick-pink eyes of rabbits,
wrinkled rooster feet.
the statistics are very scant.
on people drowning in fish-dreams.
still I want to sleep.
still you stumble
on driftwood and won't let go.
even though
I can't really remember you
I retain the memory of parts.
at night I may find your foot
in my bed, your teeth
biting into
the back of my neck.

Dreaming the Ancestors

1.

He knows me before I come.
He thinks I am moth-wings in matchlight
or the brief bite of peach skins.
His eyes float always
like dim balloons
beyond my fingertips.
Even on tiptoe I will never touch him.
His ears turn toward the sound of nightjars;
he feels them everywhere.
He traces the bison red and chalky
and shoots it full of arrows again
and again,
two teeth in his lower jaw whistling
the even note of his sympathetic magic.
He gives me candy,
full of silver stripes,
like the new money of my bones.

2.

He carves many things from wood.
Spoons for stirring the soup,
new pegs for the loom,
wheels to carry him
from one pipe to another.
He carves the bones from
the heads of rabbits.
Set upon fenceposts
they can be
decorative.
He wants to turn my skin around,
carve a kazoo from my jawbone,
play the National Anthem
as I dance over bird-beaks.

3.

When it snows we dig in together.
He gathers turnips from my hair
cauliflower from my breasts.
The two of us are gardeners,
nothing surprises us.
We pick the dark slugs
from the cellar walls,
and in spring watch
father bullfrog swallow baby sparrows.

4.

He is unthought of,
a thin knock within my bones
trying to announce itself.
The moon-blood
would form him
though now he is only fins;
and I would not recognize
his tight-curled feet,
his pig-snout,
or the unlit land he comes from.

Ice-Storm, April, 1974

That loaf of bread you baked
the slow batter taking the
form of a surprised "o"
molded by your bundt pan,
I taste the extra lemon
eating it.
The crust comes loose clinging
like skin
to the roof of my mouth.
I feel I am eating you.
You are   almost here.

Later it starts to rain.
The water grips the black twigs
on my lawn——they grow stiff,
ice-covered.
The night begins to glow
like your daughter's patent-leather shoes
on my kitchen floor,
shellac-red; already
they anticipate their pain.

Your life breaking open like the moon's laugh.
Your child still sleeping,
you've gone in the night,
left the ice on the trees.

The "Pirushke" Lady Warns Me of Going Barefoot

In a few years your arches will fall
your feet grow hooved
toes become turtles
your husband will leave.

Divorce

Your skin is coming loose.
It no longer wants any
part of you.
"Let me keep it with me," you say
"I can't survive long without it."
While inside you
the beardless ones
are already turning
on their lights.
Your skin glows like oiled parchment.
You wonder if you are still in it.

Star-Gazing, U.S.A.

  The stars are growing;
a leek garden
garden of glass-eyes.
  The stars are exploding;
sometimes we can almost
see them move.

Stars are horoscoping into our lives, surfacing
like a nose in the morning coffee.
The stranger we'll never meet,
the business deal wrangled through galaxies,
Jeane Dixon's eyes programmed like the pyramids to
intersect three million light-years away.

We're contacting the nebulous.
In the basement we've hidden a homunculus,
a warty star-struck pickle,
his beetle claws pinching us
toward the stars,
his Homeland.
We're waiting to be picked up
by Winken, Blinken and Nod,
to gorge ourselves on distance
like fresh bread.

The whole country is riding the stars,
poets see them in new ways,
relating to their lives like wristwatches.
They are shaking stars from their hair,
using stars for hearing-aids, even
tying their shoes with stars—

Everyone wants to harness a star,
belong to an inevident explosion.
We've always liked disappearing space-tricks.
This time we won't be cheated,
this time we'll repair Columbus' mistake,
riding our ships off the edge of the world.

Richard W. Thomas was born in Detroit in 1939, and is currently teaching in the Department of Racial and Ethnic Studies, College of Urban Development, at Michigan State University. He has published in numerous magazines and is included in several anthologies including *Nine Black Poets* (1968), *Facing the Whirlwind* (1971), and *Poetry of the Negro* (1970).

MSU Information Services photo

The Day the Old Man Joined the Church
(Xmas '66)

We were just sitting there,
the old man and I, listening to the choir,
early Xmas morning,

Like many other Xmas mornings
strung together almost like a
week of Xmases.

Just sitting there; mama in
the choir singing.

And I felt a tremble on
my left, a noise. And felt
an empty space happening.

Saw the old man strutting
down the aisle towards
the front.

Saw the years of love
and disbelief on mama's face

While all the folk watched
the most notorious sinner
going to meet his savior

And I stood back
struggling to keep his empty space
from spreading on me.

The Poem Is Mightier Than the Switchblade
for the Brothers in Lansing Boy's Training School

They think I gonna smuggle
a gun in
or some dynamite in my pencil
or tell you about the closets in
their skulls
or give you a recipe on how
to poison the gingerbread or
trap a cat on the john
and lynch him with toilet paper.
   But, they ain't hip that
the poem is mightier than the switchblade.

I'm just gonna read some nice poems.
Poems you can take to bed.
Poems that can fight for you
when your hands are tied

and you can put a trigger on them
if you want to.

6:00 A.M.

We're older today
by 24 hours.
Same sky, blue of it.
East, red with the murder
Of the moon,
In the coffin of night
passing
Like a tired old Negro woman
pulling fog up an alley.

Something inside focuses my attention

Something inside focuses my attention
on the trees this spring.
Watching each bare spot go
slowly yellow and green.
All the trees in the park
I know by name now.

A few are having trouble
catching hold. Some are full
green and each day try to
tell me something like babies
just learning to talk.

On the river last night
canoeing with my woman,
felt the day and night happening
out of everything. She pointed
with a scream at the
huge red moon burning behind
an apartment building.

And we both laughed at a
white couple
paddling awkwardly
down into the night, too
in love to notice.

May 3, 1969

How We Must Teach the Children

When spring comes
we must take the children
to the river
to study its ways.
They have never seen a river.

We must hold them still
in the evening.
Teach them its meaning.
Force them to find
in its setting their meaning.
They do not know the sun.

When we are naked
making love—and they come
let's not chase them away,
but let them watch
to know its meaning.
They have never seen
our people really love.

And when we laugh and are really happy
for no reason
but that we love clear rivers,
soft red evening sun, and loving
with them watching,
let's tell them that
in the end
this is what our struggle is
all about.

When I'm Alone

When I'm alone
and everybody else is doing
their own thing.
And everything is dark and
jive and the world is
laying traps.
I just sit and dig it
before I jab . . .
I just sit and wrap
my thing up tight
before jabbing . . .
then
I move out slowly
like an angel with
a do-rag on.
I move out and
before they're hip to
what's happening
the world is out cold.
Lying out, limp, because
I sat there and wrapped my
thing up tight,
because sometimes jabbing
at the wrong time blows
your whole thing. Sometimes
you got to fake a cat off balance
like instead
of jabbing,
go into a beautiful spiritual bag
and blow a cat's mind

splash his soul
all over the place

leave him chasing himself

because he can't figure out
how you got so pretty so fast!

The Worker

My father lies black and hushed
beneath white hospital sheets.
He collapsed at work;
his iron left him.
Slow and quiet he sank,
without drama or Jesus in his brain or his falling,
meeting the wet concrete floor on his way.
The wheels were still turning, they couldn't stop!
Red and yellow lights flashing, they couldn't stop!
Gloved hands twisting knobs, they couldn't stop!
And as they carried him out,
the whirling and buzzing and humming machine
                              applauded him,
lapping up his dripping iron, they couldn't stop!

James Tipton was born in Ashland, Ohio, in 1942. He lives on a farm near Elwell and teaches at Alma College. His poems have appeared in numerous magazines, and his collection of short poems, *Bittersweet,* was published recently.

Photo by Lynn Tipton

James Tipton

Winter in Elwell

Those buffalo, white, that gather in the bean field,
is it because of the winter? Head down, they huddle
together, eating the weather, swelling exploding
back into snow. No. Those were not buffalo. Giant
birds. Those giant birds that gather in the bean
field, why are they restless, why are they moving up
and down, wings bursting out of their bodies in every
direction? That woman, that woman in the bean field,
why is milk rushing out of her breasts, out of her
body, breaking over the field? That snow, that white
snow that gathers in the bean field, what is that
white snow?

Now Everyone is Writing Poems About Indians

American poets stick together. Now they are
writing prose poems about Indians. They are
tired of cardboard stars in buckets of old milk.
Now paint rushes out of their faces. It gathers
in pools around their bodies. They sit alone,
deep in their rooms, hacking their desks to
pieces, looking for poems. They have cut the
eyes out of the darkness to make light. Their
pockets are stuffed with eyes. They do not want
the darkness. They want to cry "Eureka!" But
suddenly, on stolen ponies, they are pulled back
into the darkness.

Ode

There is a door in these hands that has been
opening all night: exploding into the thin
bodies of the saved, exploding into the diaries
of New York poets, exploding into the bellies
of dead fish. Tired, I toss the book away and
walk into the kitchen. Here is another door.
It refuses to be anything but a door! Delighted,
I walk back into the bedroom, drinking beer,
humming old songs.

Exit, Pursued by a Bear

Tonight, the barn is sitting under the rain.
I sit on the bed, thinking up rivers. Suddenly
rivers rush out of my eyes, flooding
the room. I slosh through the dark to the
kitchen. I do not want those rivers. I want
a dish of blueberries, and beautiful women.

Stump Farming

Digging through these hills,
past things dying back;
and pieces of bone,
bears sleeping
when the rivers ran down—
everywhere, the stumps of trees
sinking in the slow mud.

Farming. Farming
between these stumps. Stumps
becoming centers, seats
to pass the time.

It happened this way—
an Ojibway working lumber
out of Au Sable said
one night the trees got cold
and shrunk back to seed.

No, it happened this way—
in Ohio, going back
to beginnings, a seed
with the wind
sucked out, before the sun.

There are rumors of voices
rising out of these stumps,
the way smoke rises
out of old mines,
a knowledge in these stubs
of dead tongues; but I am tired
and pass the time.

Winter Lambing

Snow circles the barn, wanting to break in,
And I long to say, "Give up old barn,
I will stay in the house, and watch the yarn
Leap out of the hands of a woman,
Into sweaters, things against the weather."

But it is late into the night. The woman
Is tucked into sleep. The body,
Like snow that has taken shape, moves
Toward the barn, slowly,
And to the animals, sleeping together.

There is little noise here at all,
Except the wind and heavy sleep of sheep
Waiting out the winter; until I hear the small,
High cry of two new lambs, and the sweet,
Strange warble of their mother.

Alive at the End of the Journey
adaptations from Basho

That old oak in the orchard
doesn't give a damn
about these plum blossoms.

Only halfway
to the ancient city
and it looks like snow.

When I heard that distant pheasant cry
I remembered how much
I loved my father and mother.

Little bird,
you will need the wings of a crane
to get between these islands.

I hired a horse
to make it over the pass.
Next time I'll hire a stick.

I keep my door locked
to everyone
but those morning glories out there.

America: The Elephant

> " . . . a movie idea I've recently had . . .
> It has its weaknesses, but I like it. I hope
> you do."
>
> -James Agee

1824 Old Bet, bought by a Somers man,
      Went mad, in Western Connecticut;
      The incarnation of Behemoth,
      Religious people shot her dead.

1885 Jumbo, beloved, being led
      Through a gap left in a long freight line
      Was on his way to bed.
      But, the unexpected express.

      Jumbo, remembering the opening back to safety,
      Ran for it, overshot, turned, and
      Head on, heavy in his skin,
      Derailed the locomotive.

1916 Tennessee: Mary,
      Berserk in a small town,
      Trampled three small men
      And met the jury.

      Strung up on a railroad derrick
      She broke it down;
      But, on a stronger derrick,
      Dangling two hours, died before that town.

1934 Grand Finale. George Balanchine. The Elephant Ballet.
      On the big night, the elephants are embarrassed,
      But dutiful, dancing in pink tights,
      Under hot lights, to Stravinsky.

      The people, between popcorn,
      Roar at this clumsy innocence,

These tired legs.
The elephants are deeply shamed.

Later that night in the dark tent,
The wisest sends out his trunk,
Sucks up a dying cigar,
And drops it in fresh straw.

The huge souls of thirty-six elephants,
Light as doves, settle
In the secret cemetery,
Back in Africa.

Eric Torgersen, born in Huntington, New York in 1943, now lives on a farm near Shepherd and teaches at Central Michigan University. He has published in numerous magazines including *Lillabulero* and *Poetry Now,* and he has published two collections of poetry: *The Carpenter* (1969), and *At War With Friends* (1972). With Paula Novotnak he edited *Poems of the People* (1970–71).

Ron Franzen photo

266

A Poem for Russell Nowak

In high school it was you who wrote darkly well.
And you knew how to do things.
I was just smart, and except for a broken front tooth
I couldn't see how anyone even recognized me.

What friends we might have been
in the town where Walt Whitman was born.

But I wouldn't say anything.

I should have written a poem in *your* yearbook.
You praised my independence.
I wrote smart advice.

What a picture you took.

You're probably a contractor.

I should have asked you to teach me how to drive.

I must have thought I had no right to anything
if the government sent us checks
and the pastor brought food before holidays.
We'd read those lousy books.

I should have been able to say Russ
I have no father.

A Story

The ending is this:
the perfect, true friend comes back
and you live in the place in the woods
as you promised each other you would.

Everyone else
in the story is parents.
They make you go to school;
you come out parents.

That's when the friend ran away.

Years in the story
you're alone.
Every new friend
ends up trying to make you eat breakfast.

Ends up getting married.

This is the place in the story
where you lost all hope.

In a Subdivision

Down the middle
of the street,
hands in pockets,
meandering
pigeon-toed—

against
the stupidity
of his changing
body—

a twelve-year-old
blonde boy,
head floating,
eyes
not looking—

far gone
into singing
just audibly
killing me
softly
with his song . . .

how quickly
I pass,
not thinking
I recognize him.

I Have Come to Be One Who Cries
for Bob Hershon

I have come to be one who cries when the plane the
guys built in shop class on the TV news is going to
fly and everybody is there, parents, little kids,
the teachers not even dressed up, the mayor and the
principal making speeches, the shop teacher saying
these are real fine boys, the guys standing around
saying it's gonna crash, putting their arms around
girls and the teachers don't stop them, the band
playing the school song while the pilot gets in and
checks everything out like you're supposed to,
finally kicks it over and taxies to the end of the
runway with a drum roll and everybody screaming
already it goes off the lift like a dragster and
takes off! and the band starts "off we go, into
the wild blue yonder" and the guys are slapping
each other five and grabbing girls and telling each
other it flies! that sonofabitch flies!

Of Birthright
for Brad Donovan

You're ready to decide
that you will run for president
when word comes:
you're chosen to be a saint.

The family is shattered
and proud;
your wife won't be ready
to speak for a while yet.

You need to be alone
with everything
you'll be giving away;
we understand.

You stare
through a tennis racket,
petting a dog that killed a rabbit once
and died.

Now: start to strip off
the clothes, success,
to be not guilty
of birthright.

My Blindness

Once I woke up in the dark and thought I was blind.
There was no light at all. There's always *some*
light.

Blind, I was calm in that perfect dark. Friends
would come for me, and I'd tell them what they had
to do. It would be all right.

I'd go back home, but with a new dignity, and I'd know
my way perfectly in the house, and even on the streets.
I'd only been gone a few years.

I'd have them read me strange books! And they'd love
my strangeness, thinking *this is what it was. We knew
there was something.* They'd loved it a little already.

There at home in my great dark I'd find a single pur-
pose, and begin.

but you know this: the light came.

Don't laugh at me. I live with so little blindness.
I've come so far, on so little blindness.

Mark Wangberg, born in Jacksonville, Florida in 1952, teaches elementary art in Saginaw. His work has appeared in *The Greenfield Review, Folio, Abraxas,* and other magazines. He is currently working on a collection of poems based upon his experiences in Nigeria.

Photo by Mark Wangberg

Love Poem

The thrust of your body
raises me on stilts—
joyous, like Jamaican boys
spearing silver fish in the moonlight.

Ibo Woman

I like the way
you move inside
those clothes
the swinging buttocks
gently riding, switching,
rolling cheeks—
and your breasts
full,
rising like knees
steeping one over the other
the nipples erect,
pouting under the
bright cloth.

Aah . . . You Ikenne Women

You grinned,
"Come Mastah"
And I bought cloth.

Weeks later
I come
Say
This is bad stuff,
Wash it and holes appear
Like borers in a cane basket.
The weave gives like an old woman's torn lips,
Like a hole in the thatched roof.
And the color
Fades . . .
Like the sun going down.
Ekuirole! Good night, Mama!
This is no way to treat customer.

It Is Beautiful, It Is Rain

I

The gray sky
gathers its heavy load,
the forehead wrinkles,
rumbles.
Then it is all rolled back,
the beautiful beads fall,
touch the red-brown earth.
Tapping like fingers,
they make small holes
in the ground,
holding the dust down for hours.

II

This time of year
the rain is never enough.
The rain comes like an old man,
the folds of his skin
hiding ten days of rain.
He walks so slowly that
we think he may die soon.
Today he could not even fill a calabash jar.
Today he just shakes the water
from his robes.

The Lizard and the Yellow Dandelion

The lizard is wearing a dandelion
between his legs,
he waves at us and spreads
his arms, blinks both eyes,
gulps twice and thinks about flies.
A small brown moth,
Thwack! . . . . .Careee . . . . .
The lizard waits for more,
the brown moth, deep inside
tickles his dandelion,
the lizard shakes with belly laughs.
He is the real comedian.
He claps for himself, bows,
nods his head twice
as if he dislikes the audience.
He swallows and the whole place
is falling off chairs,
off the leaves, off the branches.
The snail laughs right out of his thighs.
The lizard knows this is the life.
He shakes with the knowledge.
He swallows and shakes,
moves that dandelion like a dude.
He's got his eye on everyone now
and he knows he's making it.
The women all love him.
Tomorrow they will all buy dandelion pants
for their lovers.
The lizard shakes.
The dandelion hums.

Moshudi

We spar on the grass,
you swinging your white cane
laughing, scared and not knowing
which way I am coming from.
But your ears are good,
you seem to sense when I am close
enough and you give me a good whack—
I poke your belly with a long stick,
laugh and say, "You have the fat belly
of a European! It is a potato belly.
When you were little you ate so many
potatoes that they started growing
in your stomach. Now there are leaves
coming out of your ears and
your teeth look like potato eyes."

Life is ALL RIGHT

Life is ALL RIGHT
when you sit alone in the back
of a pickup,
wave at a man on a motorbike
and he smiles and waves back.

Life is all right
when you are two
sitting in the back
of a lorry
holding down the tarp
on a thousand cases
of Guinness Beer.
You think about rain
because you're in the sun.
You cover your head with

newspapers to keep
the sand out of your eyes.
It is a five minute lift to Onitsha.
The driver is Ibo.
He lets you down & gives
directions for rides to Ikenne.

Life is all right
when you are two
in the back of a Nisson
on your way home,
the last of all rides.
Life is all right
when it starts to rain,
rains like hell in fact,
and you're inside holding
the rear flap down.
You can laugh when you pass
a flatbed you almost took from Benin.
The three boys in back
all crouch behind the cab,
they are as wet as the Ore River.
They lean into the cab
trying to escape the hard rain.

Life is all right when
the driver slows down
with the rain. Life is all right
when the trees that fall
on the road are pulled & broken
quickly by men stripped
to the waist, laughing,
one man even dancing in the rain.
Life is all right.

Brother Simon Calls on Jesus Christ

Brother Simon calls on Jesus Christ
The sound of his voice rises, attacks the night.
He calls on Jesus,
He begs with his hands.
His Christian palms
are sooo open.

Tonight he is calling out the devil,
Putting his hands on the eyes of the blind,
He calls on the spot in the pupil
To disappear, to release the eye to sight.
The eye blinks blindly at him.
The pus of the blank eye is on his hand.

> He screams,
> "Believe in Jesus!
> I am calling on the power of Jesus
> To give you sight!
> I am calling on Jesus to give you sight
> Just as he gave it to Bartimaeus.
> I am calling on Jesus
> To take this evil!
> I am calling on Jesus
> To open your eyes!
> Open your eyes!
> Open your eyes and see!
> Thank Jesus for this new sight!
> Thank Jesus!
> Praise this wonderful miracle!
> Thank Jesus!
>
> I am calling on Jesus . . . "

And finally the blind are led away,
And finally the blind are left
To feel their way with tapping sticks.
And finally the blind are left blind.

Brother Simon calls on Jesus Christ
Brother Simon attacks the night.

John Woods was born in Martinsville, Indiana, in 1926 and has
for the past twenty years taught at Western Michigan University.
Widely published in literary magazines, he is the author of
several books of poetry including: *The Deaths at Paragon, Indiana*
(1955); *On the Morning of Color* (1961); *The Cutting Edge* (1966);
Keeping Out of Trouble (1968); *Turning to Look Back, Poems,
1955–1970* (1972); and *Striking the Earth* (1976).

Photo by Mara Pilatsky

Lying Down with Men and Women

When we came up from water, our eyes
drew to the front of our heads,
and we had faces. When we came up
on our knuckles, we held fruit to our mouths,
and wanted to know the chemistry
of sweetness.
            Then as we walked down
the earth's curve, trees and hills
got in our way, so we moved them
for roads and newsprint and wreckage.

Part of every day, the water mood and the tree mood
rise in our bodies, and we must
lie down a bit to honor our lost
tails and gills.
            When we lie on our backs,
we see so far away we try to give names to light,
like wild dogs we have taught
to lick our hands.
            And when we lie on our faces,
we see too close, the blank wall
at the end of the corridor.
            And so
we lie down with men and women
because we are terrified, and sometimes,
for that reason, we stand up and kill.

Making Money

The year I made more money than my father
was the year we didn't help the Hungarians.
I didn't want to help them, except in theory,
my kind of soldiering, but throwing stones
at tanks is like throwing theories at governments.
There's teeth everywhere, buried traps,
and Red tanks, patrolling the legislatures.
Suit up, Woods, and help those freedom fighters.

On the bathroom door, a pencil mark shows
when I become taller than my father. Now
it shows that Dave and Rich stand taller
than their daddy. The money comes in, all right,
a thin gas, chlorine, under the bathroom door.
I like its odor, though it makes me cough up.
My money will never make me rich, and I will
never see over the placards of young beards.
A son should not make more money than his father.

The Five Dreams

What are the five dreams of the elders?

Richard, for all his beard, has seen
mist on an autumn pond and hears
water, the color of cognac, rising
and falling in the reeds of the shallows.
He thrusts his fingers through his hair
and each nail glistens with oil.
He knows that water is giving and taking,
and that it will give and take though fists
slam shut, though the high curse
of his name burns on the door plate.

Wayne is backed against a wall of books,
and the fireplace, the *place* of fire,
reddens his forehead. In his nostrils,
two cables of air freeze, and on them
he hangs in the world. He spreads his arms,
one hand the wing of a leather testament;
the other, the one with a dead ring,
seizes a last book of poetry.
The fire eats all shadows but one.

These were two dreams of the elders.

Emily has brushed her hair forever.
Now it is earth, and pours to her feet.
Half moons glint at her fingertips,
and sand drifts from her mouth, her ears,
the corners of her eyes. She is content.
It was prophesied. Her children look in
at the windows, pale as moonlight.
Remember when they gnawed her breasts?
When she is empty, they will press her
in a book, the book of earth.

Mary knows there are dead places in her.
The doctors, well, the doctors are guessing.
Richard's kiss is dead, but we all
shed layers, and when we have been struck
too often, part of us turns to the wall.
She knows, too, that when the last cobs
of snow melt, green incoherence leaps
from eye to eye. And Wayne's ring?
Well, it turned green before it died.
She takes it off. It pings on the parquet.
The ring scar reddens. She feels better.

This is the last dream of the elders.

Each house has a room that's always locked.
This is the room of dreaming. Sometimes
it is a room of slow water where a huge eye
glares. Sometimes there is a bed
of glacial sheets, slow, slow, and in them
we can see our gill parents. And, praise God,
one night the young of us will lie down together
in a shadow of black hair. And one day
we will return, put down our cases,
pass through the room where the fist
opens, where the earth sifts, where the ring
spins to quiet. Then, we lie down in the milky,
slow sheets, when the door closes
and is a door no longer.

Everyone Born in 1926

1
Everyone born in 1926 has tried too hard.
Our grandparents occupy the ancient snows.
Our parents buy houses with ramps,
and are prepared to look Florida in the face.
We forget what they taught us of use.

Four ages make a life.
For us, fire and air are gone,
hung in bird attics, art festivals
judged by ladies with glacial hair
and matched accessories.

Earth and water, earth and water.
We drink and eat our way down to them.
Better not stand too long in one place,
friend, parts of you are going home early.

If you are the secretary
of the class of 1944, take this note:
we die three times: once from the mother,
once from the father, and once
from ourselves.

1926 has its people everywhere.
A molecular summoning in black water,
blind, swimming from safety lines,
we took electric messages.
We drew up like fish from the old bed.
Fathers, mothers,
fishing, telling of light and grain futures,
pulled white and breathing creatures
into the drying winds,
on the day the clocks started
to stop.

Everyone Born in 1926

2

Remember, it was John Woods who told you
  in April the garden would leap up
    like a brown cat, spin twice,
  and come down bristling green
with news from the tail.

Jefferson Blount Woods' son John
  thought he knew every riff
    of black Ecclesiastes
  and the cast in the eye
of walletsized, handtinted holyghosts.

Stand beside me, Professor Woods, let's see
  if you've grown an inch
    since you gathered up your roots
  like hair spats and came down
in the compost of the next county.

It was Woodsey-boy and no almanac
  who shivered all seventeen while the girls
    went to dress for the dignity
  of the Hill Top Motel
and never came back, too bad and thank God.

It was J. Warren Woods who ran
  until he was red and drank
    until he was white and blew
  until he was blue in the face
some mad tale of Nutter's Hill and kites.

The line waiting for grades can peel off.
  The line wanting advice can shuffle itself.
    Those wanting sugar tits can suck,
  and pre-post neurotic women
can carry off their couches on their backs.

It's my home stand, people, I'm holding sway.
  I know my own mind or whatever
    wills green ears in the shrubbery.
  Come in and howdy the top part
because the roots have a one-way to the elements.

You had your chance to ring my nose,
  bell my tail and bug my sperm,
    brand the neck of my laundry
  and cauterize the frank blood
of my stare. Johnny was here but he left.

INDEX OF TITLES AND FIRST LINES

Poem titles are in roman type and first lines in *italics*.

One-hundred-sixty-five poets answered the call for poetry sent out in 1975 by editors Conrad Hilberry, Kalamazoo College; Herbert Scott, Western Michigan University; and James Tipton, Alma College. Of these, thirty poets were selected for presentation in this volume, which Wayne State University Press publishes in cooperation with the Michigan Council for the Arts as a Bicentennial project.

The manuscript was prepared for publication by Barbara Woodward. The book was designed by Richard Kinney. The typeface for both the text and display is Palatino.

The text is printed on Bookmark paper. The hardcover edition is bound in Joanna Mills' Linson 2 cloth over binders boards; the paperback edition is bound in Simpson Lee's Teton cover. Manufactured in the United States of America.